DEMENTIA BLOG

SUSAN M. SCHULTZ

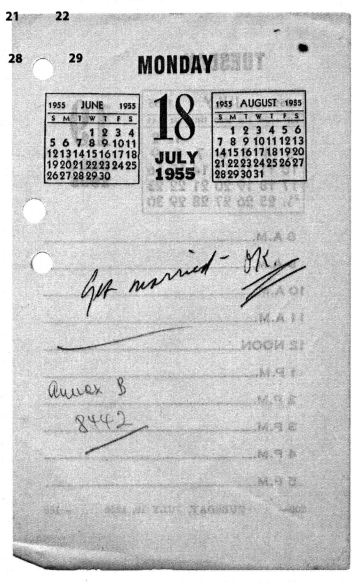

MONDAY

1955 JUNE 1955							18	1955 AUGUST 1955						
S	M	T	W	T	F	S		S	M	T	W	T	F	S
			1	2	3	4			1	2	3	4	5	6
5	6	7	8	9	10	11	JULY	7	8	9	10	11	12	13
12	13	14	15	16	17	18		14	15	16	17	18	19	20
19	20	21	22	23	24	25	1955	21	22	23	24	25	26	27
26	27	28	29	30				28	29	30	31			

SINGING HORSE PRESS — 2008

"Susan M. Schultz's *Dementia Blog* is as astonishing as it is tragic. Following the odd form of the blog, which is written forward in time but read backwards, it charts the fragmented disorienting progression (if this is the word) of her mother's dementia. Well schooled in the unpersonism of post-modern innovative poetry, ('dementia destroys the self, but that destruction is oddly, horribly, poetic,' she says), Schultz sees through her family's personal tragedy to the profound social and philosophical implications of the unraveling of sense and soul: a deranged nation, so unmoored from coherence that it is unable to feel the difference between political rhetoric and the destructiveness of war. Full of intimate personal detail, *Dementia Blog* sweetly and sadly unwinds itself into timelessness."

— Norman Fischer

"I'm fascinated by Susan M. Schultz's *Dementia Blog*. In it, no pronoun has a single antecedent but all of them float in the same cybervapor we all float in. 'I envy the lyric poet,' Schultz writes. Who doesn't? For Schultz, the lyric poet is the altered perspective with the quote marks missing. *Dementia Blog* is a phone calling home to say, I know I still love you but it's hard, said without quote marks — so anyone might be speaking. And the answer comes back, Log on and look in. Everything is here. The emotion pressing out, and the world pressing in."

— Mary Jo Bang

"Published shortly after his death in 1946, Lásló Moholy-Nagy's *Vision in Motion* surveys in panoramic sweep a range of art forms and methods with the aim of 'add[ing] to the politico-social a *biological* "bill of rights" asserting the interrelatedness of man's fundamental qualities, of his intellectual and emotional requirements, of his psychological well-being and his physical health.' Toward the end of his volume, Moholy-Nagy illustrates how various modernist experiments in literature and poetry might be productively aligned with (among other things) the writings of 'psychologically disturbed patients,' which he examines under the heading 'the psychotics.'

The latent determinism at work here should perhaps give us pause, and yet Moholy-Nagy's emphasis, finally, is on instructional content: what can be learned, and how best to learn it. Sixty years later, working in a new and newly ubiquitous expressive form, the blog, Susan M. Schultz tracks her mother's growing dementia, drawing parallels between this personal tragedy and the fraught geopolitical reality within which it unfolds. *Dementia Blog* is the transposition of Schultz's blog, written over a period of six months, to the ostensibly more stable confines of print, and as the form dictates, one reads the earliest entries last.

As a daughter, Schultz proves a painfully keen observer of her mother's plight. As a poet and a teacher, Schultz inquires deeply into the relationship between familial bond and autonomous identity, between the capacity to remember and the necessity to forget, between the severe demands of art and the equally severe limitations of mental illness, between words and the alternately stable and tenuous interiorities that would make sense of them. In the process, Schultz demonstrates how the emotional and intellectual are a function both of desire and circumstance, how we are ineluctably bound together under the sign of the human even as social and institutional and biological forces would tear us asunder.

A haunting work."

—Joe Amato

"The world observed by Susan M. Schultz zigs when it should zag, pops when it should lock. 'Secret memos leak' from Rumsfeld's war room, while Schultz's mother can't remember where her grandchildren came from. All is wrong with the world, and yet: 'The green trees blaze in yellow light, the purple clouds. Frog song cedes to dove song.' Writing both aids and obstructs memory, the memory her mother is losing, the memory our nation never seems to have; and the poem is a closed system. Half outrage and half true love, half poem and half op-ed, this stunning work is an extended cry for decency, for power of attorney, the world over."

—Kass Fleisher

Mahalo nui loa to the editors of publications in which sections of *Dementia Blog* have been published: Claudia Keelan and Chris Arigo (*Interim*), Joel Chace and Heather Thomas (*5-trope*), Pam Brown and John Tranter (*Jacket*), Frances Kruk and Redell Olson (*how2*), Eric Chock and Darrell Lum (*Bamboo Ridge*), Lee Gutkind (*The Best Non-Fiction Writing 2007*), Dennis Philips and Martha Ronk (*New Review of Literature*), and William and Lisa Howe (Slack Buddha Press).

ISBN 0-935162-41-0

Singing Horse Press
3941 Gaffney Court
San Diego, CA 92130

Singing Horse Press books are available from the publisher at **singinghorsepress.com** or from Small Press Distribution (800) 869-7553 or at **spdbooks.org**.

To my mother's neighbors and ohana, in particular Milt and Eleanor Werthmann, Maureen and Pablo Falo, Connie Dixon and the late Ernie Dixon;

to the good women at Ann E. O'Neil Care Options for the Elderly and Disabled, especially Karen Kelly and Linda Mazaway, the entire staff of Arden Courts of Fairfax, also Sara George, Mohama Foriwaa, Amina Buyaii, Bessie Tompkins, Dr. Anthony Rimicci, and Elizabeth Wildhack, Esq.;

to Lissa Wolsak, Anne Dewey, Anastasia Hagar, Miriam Lewin, Tiare Picard, Leonard Schwartz, Laura Mullen, Linh Dinh, Norman Fischer, Deborah Meadows, Lisa Koehler, Sheri Swaner, Janet Bowdan, Rachel Loden, Jon Morse, Kristin Pelzer, Catherine Taylor, Ursula Chappell, Laura Lyons, Marie Hara and other readers of the blog in real or past time; to Joseph Boyden for "seven eight nine"; to Lisa Smith and Dave Taylor and Josh, Gini, Sammy and Meera Dietrich for sanctuary and good conversation; to Diane Weible and Aaron Belz for the 2006 World Series; to Jeff Carroll for the political links; and to Ikaika Hashimoto for proofing;

to the students of English 613, Fall, 2006, and to Goro Takano and his demented narrator, Lulu;

to Paul Naylor, who shares the profound experiences of Alzheimer's and poetry; to Gaye Chan, cover artist and Tinfish comrade;

to Anne and Brad Waters, in-laws extraordinaire; to my cousins and to Aunt Gretchen; above all to Bryant, who flew thousands of miles to organize my mother's house (that was the very least of it); and to Sangha and Radhika who love Grandma Wawa;

to all of you I offer my deepest thanks.

Dementia Blog: A Fore and After Word

I kept a travel blog over the summer of 2006 for family and
friends. *We did this and we did that* filled up the month of July,
when we were (as they say) "abroad." As August began, we
arrived in northern Virginia, where my mother lives. She was still
at home then, but lived there with difficulty, as her dementia had
progressed (if progress it was) until she could not care for herself,
but refused to (could not) admit that fact. The blog turned serious
and became a prose poetic project. Dementia destroys the self, but
that destruction is oddly, horribly, poetic. My mother was crossing
paths with my children (5 and 7), who were developing maturity and
independence even as she was losing it. But the processes were not
utterly dissimilar, those of loss and gain. So I began to record what
I saw. What had seemed awkward about the blog, the way in which
it's written forward but read backwards, suddenly made sense as
a *form* in which to work on the process of memory and forgetting.
Whatever is confusing about reading the story backwards is intended
by the form. The confusions offered by the form are similar (or at
least apt metaphors) to the confusions of dementia.

There is also a political content to this blog. During the time it was
written, the Bush administration was pushing us closer to the abyss.
The administration's uses of the language seemed, to this reader,
demented. The split between reader and author, between the person
who suffers (or causes to suffer) and the person who reads about it,
forms a significant part of my "plot."

I dedicate this blog to my mother's many friends, to my family and
to everyone for whom dementia is a family and/or national event.
Their losses of memory cause us to lose our loved ones; our loss of
memory may cause us to lose our nation.

Wednesday, January 03, 2007

--The famous person of the day is Jim Bakker. Michael asks: *Does anyone remember Jim and Tammy Faye Bakker from the 80s?* The supervisor's mother used to send them money. They stole it. *Do you think people of the cloth should be held to a higher standard?* The supervisor says they're just flesh and blood, like her. That's right, says the woman whose sweatshirt has grandchildren's names on it. (*When I make 'em, I make 'em*, she says, lifting her breasts with her hands. *I guess I shouldn't say that.*) Yesterday she was Woman 1. Woman 2 ignores her today.

--Michael is from West Virginia. He is large and wears black pants every day, a brown jacket. His beard is thin, as is his hair. He says he has no idea what time it is, or if it's morning or afternoon.

--*Why are we talking about this?* Yes! *They should all just forget about it and pray to the Lord.* That's what I do. *I don't want to talk about this.* Listen to the context of the entire conversation, Emma tells her.

--Michael's wife arrives; she does not have cancer. They leave. Lina takes over. She says something about Catholic priests. *We do not want to talk about this. Not all Christians.*

--They decide to sing instead. *God bless America, land that I love, stand beside her and guide her...*

--Let's write a poem:

The Christmas tree is a song.
Roses are red.

--*Is this what you expected?* the grandmother asks. This was not what she expected. Another asks what I think of the "clientele."

--The woman who wears silk dresses moans. She sits in the back and cries. *You mean you can't tell me that, Christine; but you went to Juilliard!* Next door she cries again, sings Barney's song: *You love me, I love you.*

--The woman in the festive red sweater asks if I'm a professor. *I am a professor, too* she says, her pale eyes wide. *Health administration. Pitt, San Bernardino--that's in San Bernardino. Get your mother some cough drops; she has a cold.*

--The woman who wore no shoes is wearing them, black canvas shoes with white rubber on the bottom. She does not sit still. She places her hands on my shoulders, leans over, whispers *you're red hot.* The angry woman next to me says *stay away from me, I'm not like that!* when the woman with the canvas shoes approaches her. She walks in and out, sits and gets up. She speaks, but her subject is not ours.

--The woman who looks most European enters in a striped top; she could be sailing. She sits next to my mother, pushes her chair forward, then back. Lina tells her to stop. STOP. She pushes back until the chair is lodged against another. She keeps pushing. I pull a chair up beside my mother and sit. My mother smiles.

--One of the two black residents was a gym teacher. *I'd just pull out my whistle now and tell them all to stop!* She carries a kleenex box wherever she goes.

--The memory boxes hold faces that smile out at you. Mental archeology gets you closer; sometimes the name gets you there, where they were before they forgot and their skin forgot and we who did not know them then cannot know them now. *She is an angel, your mother. She always smiles at me.* Memory boxes keep families close in some time before this one. Loved ones hold each other, cradle babies. One photo is from 1958; it says so. That was the woman who squeezes my shoulders. That was the inappropriate man who gives the women flowers, talks about their lust. That was the woman who hates her name, with a family that must have had one. That was the man in overalls who puts his head down at lunch, even when he eats. That was Dr. French, who cannot stay awake. *Name me one song from the musical Oklahoma.* They all begin to sing.

posted by Susan at 7:58 PM 0 comments

Tuesday, January 02, 2007

--The woman who is not wearing shoes comes up behind me and places her hands on my shoulders. She squeezes them. I turn and ask her name. She does not know.

--The heavyset man with a Virginia teeshirt comes to feed his wife lunch each day. She hasn't been able to say how she feels for six years. *But she's a sweetheart. She's very sweet.* He pulls out a pocket comb and pulls it through her short white hair.

--Woman 1: *Tell him you want him to sit on your lap. Tell him you don't want him to sit on your lap. OUCH! What did you just do?* Woman 2: *I just pinched you. You stuck it out there for me.* She reaches out, pinches the first woman's breast again.

--*Do you have grandchildren?* I ask the woman with the "I love grandchildren" sweatshirt. *I use them up!* I ask how many grandchildren she has. *All is not right up here,* she answers, pointing to her head.

--*I can laugh at everything,* says Woman 1. *That's the problem.*

--Woman 2 points to her head and nods toward Woman 1.

--The woman who hates her own name stumbles when she gets past the railing. I'm holding my mother's hand. I ask if she too would like a hand. *I don't need any help!* she says. *I don't know how I talked to her,* she tells my mother, *but I get angry at people who want to help me.* Don't be that way, my mother says.

--My mother's skin is too small for her, is brown, its ridge lines steep. There are white spots on the brown. Her ankles are a rough white. Her hair is pulled up, curled at the top. Her shoulders stoop, but she skitters ahead until I speed up. *She is very special,* says Woman 1, *and you're just like her.*

--The woman who hates her own name tries to carve her napkin with a knife. Each reads "Country Lane." It's so she'll know which is hers. The woman who gives her lunch says she'll help. She takes the napkin, begins to carve until fade out.

--The woman with the loud sweater comes after me, says she has a cold (meaning my mother, who coughs). *I spent a thousand dollars trying to get over my cold. The only thing that worked was cough drops. Get your mother cough drops.*

--The woman who collects dolls (one hangs around her neck) says her husband was in Hawai`i during the war. She wonders if I was there during the war, though she knows something is wrong with her question. *Not that war.* The woman who hates her name has taken her napkin, too.

--Xavier is in his early 20s. Xavier attended Bible School, earned his MA in psychology. Xavier tosses a yellow ball back and forth with everyone in a green chair. *Dr. French, you need to wake up!* Xavier reads out loud from the newspaper. 3000 killed in Iraq. A faint gasp. The man who is most competent opines we must get out of Iraq, there's no other way. Doesn't like Clinton, though. Monica Lewinsky (*we'll tell you about her later*). Xavier says Gerald Ford is lying in state. He died? Xavier asks how you'd cook a turkey. He asks what goals they have. *How many Afghans will you sew?* Finish one, start another.

posted by Susan at 6:49 AM 0 comments

Sunday, December 31, 2006

--I grew up on a pig farm, which is where I met HIM.
--Minnesota, Minnesota. I don't remember where in Minnesota.
--Are you just going to stand there in front of me?!
--Kick him out. Kick him out.
--How do you keep rabbits out of a garden? Shoot 'em!
--People get together with their families for dinner.
--Gone With the Wind.
--Poland. Ireland. England. Ireland.
--See, she's trying to get her hands in my pants. Sheila, too.
--Do you have change for a quarter? Can you get in the vending machines?
--Is this the way we go?
--I hate my name.
--I don't know if I like my name or not. It's my name.
--My son travels a lot. He's single.
--She's my girlfriend: see!
--Did I ask you for change earlier? Do you have any more?

--She's very sweet and very proper, the nurse tells me. *I thought maybe she was a socialite.*

--People clapped as the hearse passed down Washington Street, Alexandria. Someone waved in one of the other vehicles. A second hearse went by. That one had a flag inside it. *Our long national nightmare is over*, he had said.

--My mother smiles to see me. *Sweetie.* She sits in a chair in a large room and she turns her ankles this way and then that. Lifts her legs below the knee. We go to lunch and she smiles. I show her kids' photos and she smiles. Hands them back. *Is she always so quiet?* I ask the nurse. *Yes.* Michael, who initiates the ankle twists, says she talks to him. She remembers why she liked her husband, he says, and she graduated from the University of Iowa. *Did she teach at Langley High School?* he'd asked earlier, and I said no. She does not say her home town, or how to keep the rabbits out, or how to grow roses;

nor does she speak the name of a best-seller or sing the song the television brings.

--Two men and a knife. A pregnant girl. The scheming older woman. Stanley on a boat, Stella serving coffee on a tray. Clearly, the plot is dark. Someone will get hurt. And yet they sing, on deck, on the rocky shore, to themselves and to each other. This was before West Side Story. When Americans were wholesome, did not seduce each other at clam bakes while their songs entered the happy place.

--*She's in her happy place*, the nurse says. *We'd all like to be there. People come and go, but nothing affects them much. It's all the same.*

--*What are they talking about? We can't hear the movie. Be quiet!*

--Poetry or poetic prose. Sequence or unraveling of. Prose or text message. Forward, then back. The writing dances, a child beside the canal, its green water not yet inviting. Failure to thrive. Two of them died right after they came. She did not. Failure to fail to thrive is life. Life is a happy place.

posted by Susan at 6:46 AM 0 comments

Saturday, December 23, 2006

--*Bad year for empire*. Occlusions of memory. Do not tell us
what you did in Vietnam or Panama or the Philippines, Cuba or
Cambodia. We have chosen to tivo those out. Shiites "reorganize"
neighborhoods. Once mixed, they're now "purified." *We've created
a culture of dependency in Iraq*, the governor opines. If only they'd
grow up to be like us. He actually likes to hang out with his parents.
The journalist compares Iraqis to American Indians. Forgetting is not
easy; there is blood on its hatchet, too.

--In her year of greatest dependency, she lashed out at others. [Cross
species metaphor erased here.] In her year of forgetting, she took on
new memories like clothing to cover the disfigurations. In her year
of assuming new facts, she forgave the president his lies (*he's not so
bad; don't be so hard on him*!).

--New rules from China: no one with a facial disfiguration can adopt
a Chinese baby. (Provisions also against obesity, singleness, age and
anti-depressants.)

--I live in `Ahuimanu, Temple Valley, Kāne`ohe, on Hui Kelu
Street, near the cemetery and the McDonald's, windward side of the
Ko`olaus, mauka of the highway, parking lot 5. *Were they part of the
British empire?* he asks about Nepal. They gave their soldiers to the
British and kept their land.

--She writes about Jerusalem. Old Arab man attacked by young Arab
men. Enter the Israeli police. Blame put where it always is. Hers
is not a defense of empire, but a puncturing of story that fails to
acknowledge particular fact. Not a call to action, but to observation.
Dangerous to see amoeba in the microscope when there is the sea!

--The brain is wider than. Oh for an ounce of your poetry's acid, Emily, to sear through this empire's rigid grammar.

posted by Susan at 10:58 AM 0 comments

Thursday, December 21, 2006

--Her friends' notes come to me: *I was in surgery, have bad diabetes and I'm sorry we lost touch; my daughter is away and everyone else is dead and I tried to call, but the phone was disconnected.* Do not expect her to write back, I write back.

--The hikers were missing for a week on the mountain. One called from his cave, said his friends were on airplanes, or at home in Dallas. Hour after hour the mountain rose a vivid white on the television; black dots were rescuers. He was found, his cell phone sodden, testimonial photos in a disposable camera. The story cannot end on television, is dropped.

--Refuse closure, the poet insists. Language, like the mountain, offers no RSVP to our insistence that it hold us like a cave or a perfect sentence. Techniques of fiction offer tension released in an ending. The couplet demands we change our lives, but tells us how. Buy a map of the city, the syllabus says. I dream they will not let me finish my degree; I dream my life has no direction now, which is then. A dream of openness disguised as anger. My mother's rage at being told her laundry had been done again, by her. *Again* the angry word that cannot acknowledge the end.

--Sangha doesn't want *Harry Potter*; it's too scary. Nor *The Legend of Sleepy Hollow*. In his hands, Santa becomes an action figure.

--If the story refuses to end, if the story exhausts the frame called "story," if the story is about the dissolution of story (what we cannot remember is no longer story, but Sappho), if the story is remnant, ruin, then what holds us to it? My mother's life a loaded one, her words clues, symptoms to a foregone opening. The scholar translates death laments. But what do you call the lament that lacks death?

--Holding patterns. Which is the alpha word, the one to govern its phrase? Can one exist without the other?

--And if the lack of ending does not yet suggest openness? When the failure to die does not open the possibility of (re)birth?

--Like Jesus, I tell the kids, Santa is someone who only gives, does not receive. At the corner, an inflated Santa towers over the plastic holy family. Down the hill, he turns and turns in a plastic bubble. The mean man has the most decorations. During the day, Santas lie flat, lacking air. Birth before death certain, resurrection into this myth of goods and services. Those we love shall die only by degree.

posted by Susan at 10:46 AM 0 comments

Saturday, December 16, 2006

--*Are the programs any good?* I ask. *Not really,* she answers, in character. *I'm so glad to hear you're doing well.* Her voice is muddy; she doesn't know where it went.

--She was as surprised to see us on the second day as on the first. Knowledge is the memory you've done this at least once before. Prancing through the snow, in a one-horse open sleigh. Sangha sings: *Har-ry Pot-ter's com-ing to town!*

--The senator began to stutter, then recovered his words (hear the tape at cnn.com). He lay on his couch, unable to move his body or his mouth. The president *sleeps better at night than you might imagine.* Talk of *doubling down* the troops. Christmas bombing. Grammar as stricture, as ligament, as joint that aches when it bends. Incursion. Which side of the river are you on, and how did you get there? What you say will be used against you, no matter what it is. *I'd like to see them so they can take me home.*

--The art of lying is one of omission. The lie is lyrical, says less than it means, in as few words as possible. Taut prosody, the art not of losing but of making up. To cover over with paint; to mend a friendship's wound; to invent whole cloth.

--Parent as editor. She says: *There are only three smart kids in my class* (she's one of them). The parent says: *They're probably all smart; just not in Japanese.* She says: *There are only three smart kids in my class, but the others are good in other things.* Ethical orthodontics (she loses actual *tooths*).

--*Why can't my sister live here?* [Because she has another mother.]

--The defense secretary is sent off with "fond memories." *The best friend I've ever had* (the vice president); *The best defense secretary in American history* (the vice president). The president will not entertain any ideas that lead to defeat. *We will attain victory in Iraq.*

--The cat attacks his phantoms, hurtles into the palm's fronds. Once a day he gallops around the house, attacks the chair, the carpet on the stairs. Once a day he confuses his world with another, more dangerous, and once a day he launches pre-emptive strikes upon it. Sangha finds empty claw casings sometimes. The cat sleeps better than you'd think.

posted by Susan at 11:26 AM 0 comments

.

Thursday, December 15, 2006

--Amber answers when I call to ask what I owe to Arden Courts. Last
night there was a Christmas party. The musician played an inflatable
guitar; they all danced. It was wild! *Did my mother have a good
time?*

--Incontinence (not yet). Anxiety (always). Loss of (you name it).
Patter's muses. Old age is excess, the more than fits, the less than can
be controlled. Less than remembered is more than sustains us. What
we have is what we were, to this point. *Are we there yet?* No, here.
Zeno works in time, if not space.

--Laura Bush claims the media fails to present the good side of Iraq.
Rumsfeld says if you fly over Iraq you'll see it's not all burning.
Parse without parsimony. Untruth as excess, as the more than is true.
We admit defeat, but press on the temporary tattoo of a rose thrown
at troops "on the ground."

--*Improvised explosive device*. Coltrane's favorite things.

--I show Sangha photos of his aunts in Cambodia. He says he
remembers the smaller woman on the left in the pink shirt. The
significance of photographs in adoption narratives. *Their sister was
your birth mother,* I tell him. *She died.* Those who remain to be
photographed do not smile. Their faces are tired, foreheads creased.
Speedboat on a river in Takeo province. Field beside the water. The
sisters appear again. "You could not remember her," I say; "you were
a tiny baby." Then let go. If he says he remembers, he does.

--There is a photograph of a photograph of a half-sibling and cousin.
Sangha leaves to find his sister. At dinner she asks, "when will we go
see where Sangha was born?"

--I tell Hongly that everyone clearly tried to find a place for the baby, but failed. *All the stories are like that,* he says.

--An acquaintance sends an email ad for *The Stork Market: America's Multi-Billion Dollar Unregulated Adoption Industry.* "2. an in-depth report on the international market where children are the commodity being bought and sold to the highest bidders including pedophiles with prices based on quality (i.e. age, skin color) of the merchandise and set as high as 'desperate' consumers continue to be willing to pay."

--The boy (was he 10, 12?) attached himself to me at Bal Mandir. He smiled, he followed. He was like a cat that rubs you as if to say "I'm not feral." We toured the orphanage, met the women who cared for the children, gave them combs and lotions. They smiled, and we. The boy held to me, without touching, walked the corridors with me. Then he was gone. I turned toward a room packed with babies, and we were gone, out the front door of a cold former palace. In the car I wept. *What's the matter?* Ramesh asked Bryant. By the waters of.

--Geneva, where I visited my father by the lake. Swiss watches. Time as an elegant object. It passes, marked by works that do not fail. It passes, contained in a gold case. If time is not worth much, the watch will be.

posted by Susan at 11:07 AM 0 comments

Wednesday, December 13, 2006

--Take the "con" out of confession. We need time to parse the
report, said the White House spokesman. In this space I confess
my mother's life; wonder why I assume that right (or wrong). *He
was member of both reading groups: the Marxist and the Christian.*
When I rehearse the words *I am feeling low because I am so
homesick,* to what extent do I appropriate, and to what purpose?
Luna on the Rubber Stamp Plantation, she reiterated her desire that
mail be returned to sender, not to the deceased party whose address
now fails. There's no place in which she could be content, though
here she becomes my content, the muse of her dementia a weak sister
to her elders, those who whispered an angel's tongue in another's ear.
Ear and ethos, ethos and the recasting of my mother's words to mean
something to us, though not to her. The desire to be useful. She wants
her body given to science. I give her words' bodies to art, though she
signed no release.

--I edit out the day to day, give privacy to its inhabitants. That leaves
thoughts scattered as if unrelated to the others. They are there. I give
them back.

--*It is the greatest poem, and it failed.*

---We wave our arms side and back, usher in the sweet ramblings
of a man we only see on a large screen. He sings to us. The guitar
comes in, its odd notes shrieked through two dozen speakers. His
finger makes a sound loud enough to bang your chest. The reporter
calls them brain surgeons. In the act of decadence he assumes a voice
of reason, nay the name of love. It could not be more paradoxical,
kind.

--To write about others without making of them stick, stock figures.
The one who learns language, the other whose teeth sprout, the third
who shepherds them to school. She who writes about them loves
them, but in the writing loses feeling. Words are not to be touched,

not here on the screen. There is no velvet on the word. It is dark and hard and composes itself letter by letter, the kind chiseled into lead or pixellated for your reading comfort. He laughed that I did not know "Pilates" as exercise, rather than Roman king.

--Who knows the difference between Sunni and Shia earns a trip to Iraq or place in the study group that pronounces the word "failure" as it must be pronounced. We are well past enunciation now. *We will achieve victory.*

--The hen clucks, the rooster calls. The cat meows from the grass. Birds chatter that he is near. Call distraction for what it is. It may be our lives, but that means we are missing things. The aquarium bubbles, a distant television hums. Key clack.

posted by Susan at 4:51 PM 0 comments
About Me

Name:Susan
Location:Kāne`ohe, Hawai`i

Previous Posts

Archives

Powered by Blogger

Thursday, December 07, 2006

--She says my life sounds fragmentary. I say fragments must be set down to see where their edges meet. He says he "throws his eye" at the books I sent. I say in English we do not throw our eyes, we cast them. Whiz of the line, kerplunk. Your glance is a hooked fish; you will draw him back in. He and you will drown in fullest air.

--They wrote of seams, of writing as a rough sewing. Canvas or skin, brush stroke scar.

--Sangha asks how to spell "broomstick." He speaks of walking through magic walls, writes that Harry loves "Hermione," that he wants to walk to the "castle," that he feels how little boys feel who have "magic" powers. The "cupboard" was his orphanage.

--Use the word "and" to mean as many things as it can, then move on to "or."

--Operation Forward Together. Operation Desert Storm. Operation Just Cause. Operation Enduring Freedom. And in my theater: Operation (Cult of) Overwork, Operation Disseminated Gossip, Operation Betrayal Guesswork, Operation Control Freak, Operation Drama Queen/King.

--Emma calls to say mom has pneumonia in her lower left lung.

--Radhika makes her own connect-the-dots pictures. Which come first, lines or dots? In a desert country, there are dots for cities, very few river lines. Anbar Province: 11 Americans killed yesterday by IEDs that can pierce a tank's skin. *This is an elephant!* And this discarded metal. Open it up and see all the people.

II.

--To avoid fragments, join together mother's pneumonia with the
IEDs in Anbar with the operations that leave orphans in cupboards
with the boy who would fly from them on his broomstick with the
fish who makes his progress back to sea, away from the rod and line,
line that leads us to the page-end, ragged edge where we find (this
other morning exercise) haole privilege on-line with the metaphor
of the back-of-the-bus turned on its head, where the haole sits at the
back and forward together those who are not haole assume the front
seat position in this geometry. I have heard those words in those
subject/object positions, yes, but what of other sentences, those that
refuse closure, open to offer me a middle seat? I will not let go this
contested beauty. For each sentence admit the possibility of another,
and another. If you are the guilty settler of one sentence, change your
noun and verb. The adjectives will follow.

posted by Susan at 11:37 AM 0 comments

Sunday, December 03, 2006

--Oh, not much really. They had a hard time finding me today. Many women feel rage at this time of life; others weep at the drop of a pin (cushion). Radhika looks for letters on the floor. The alphabet is neat, like gin. In order, it fails to mean.

--Secret memos leaked. The mean level of water in Windward streams before the tunnels, before the storms, before the pineapple fields, before the resorts, did not include storm surges. The defense secretary gets a medal; he smiles. The defense secretary says we are not succeeding in Iraq. He says pull troops into Baghdad. Baghdad says three cars exploded at once, killing dozens. One man looks for his son at the morgue. One man becomes a hundred men, a hundred women, grandmothers, sisters, brothers, their shoulders hooked in premature mourning.

--She writes that her understanding of love is "premature."

--Write what you know. Know what you see on television, its broken choreography of axles, car tucked beneath a house, ponds of blood, sentences diagrammed and broken, spent arrows, solace within the chaos she says must be resolved in order.

--X-rays disrobe the traveler. She sings beyond the genius of airport security. The shore is there to stop us.

--To write late is to revise. To revise is to contain a life. The first time many of us enter the house of an ordinary African American, the famous writer notes, is within the pages of this picture book about Katrina. $90.00 plus shipping. How will you read? As native, settler, or as tourist?

--The Crimean war rages above the bed, and Washington still surveys his slaves on the near wall. Out the back window, Waikiki. He sings all the way to W each time he puts his spelling words in order. According to many historians, W. is the worst in history.

--She sounded distant, her breath shallow. She did not say she was homesick. She told Radhika she couldn't hear. Sangha said he was eating. It's not the image that's hard to face but the sound. Dissolution of language, not by syllables but by what is no longer contained in or by them. What she no longer says takes more time not to say. How it seems not the dissolution of her language, but ours. What I can still say is simply not received. The receiver is gone; so are my words, whatever they tried to mean. How I tried to make them mean. Context, not form, breath not page. *She is a page poet.*

posted by Susan at 12:16 PM 0 comments

Sunday, November 19, 2006

--Nothing left except loss of house. *I'm homesick.* Quiet on the line.
"Children are the envy of mystics," my student writes. The old are
not the envy of children, despite the blur of this with that (where *this*
is *here* and *that* is *not*). She fell in love with Lorca. Radhika uses
the word *because* as an intensifier. Sentences built not on logic but
performance. Readily they include positive with the negative: *I did
not paint, I did.* Asks questions to which she knows the response.
I will ask Milt for a ride home is an assertion we never answer. Her
voice hangs and falls, drags and drops. Quiet, for silence suggests
the idea of quiet, where quiet occurs without idea. *I understand how
you feel* is empathy and avoidance. In family, distance is boundary
is the love that will not say what hurts before it's forgotten. "Keep
her happy" is insufficient at its core, but who would say the truth
instead?

--How he did what he did, *if* he did it. The conditional sells. Pretend
you are at Costco, where you abhor the goods. Pretend the goods
are allegorical, dressed in sack cloth, pilgrims walking toward
enlightenment, not the paper towels. Pretend you are Very Goods,
aiming for towels with justice in your heart. Pretend there is an end
to capital, a cessation of cash flow, a flaw in the cash register. Pretend
there is circulation of goods without the flow, the flaw. Her shirts
were made in Cambodia.

--Take back his Nobel Prize for Genocide. He says we cannot win in
Iraq, but we should not leave. Peace with honor. The secret plan. His
gift for grab. The German grave.

--The men in blue are invested in the game they judge. Value
appreciates or they—and those who play the game—lose. The
system is closed. There are ethical considerations in any closed
system. But we cannot say: *he failed to reach first before the throw,
but his effort was so good we will award him the base anyway.*

--The poem is a closed system, no matter its length. To return to a closed system, with a view to keeping it open, leaves what we call "a publishing history." We can open the system for only so long before the buzzer sounds and the system shuts of its own will, not ours. The blog assigns my entries a time, but it is always wrong. Not just by zone, but by my clock. This will matter only to one who writes by the clock.

--Minutes matter in a murder, or in a poem. This is not to say that murder and poems are analogous, though as Stevens wrote, *poetry can kill a man*. That is one abstract murderer.

--Fox retains the "homicide bomber" as its agent of destruction. Rhetoric is not susceptible to democracy, only to the bottom line.

--If you play with pronouns, do not simply find and replace. If you mean to say *I*, do not substitute the pronoun *they* unless you mean to include *us*. If you cannot find *us*, do not make us *we*. If you invent community, it may invent you back. If you feel excluded, do not use words of inclusion. If you use words of inclusion, erase the *I*. If you write lyric, make sure to balance your life.

--Does she remember your name? When did she stop bathing? When did she begin to get so angry? When did she begin to confuse the present with the past? When did she begin to look for her mother? When did she stop?

--Ethical question #513: During the showing of *The OJ Trial: Unanswered Questions*, were the ads *for* Darfur, or was their purpose other?

--What does a bruised conscience most resemble? *I feel bad that the bruises were because of me, but she would have looked back in the middle of the night anyway.*

--I don't know how this section relates to the one that precedes and follows it.

posted by Susan at 11:46 AM 0 comments

Sunday, November 12, 2006

--What I do not say to her: *this is your home now. The other is gone.*

--The poem is a domestic space. (In these my middle years I cannot think beyond it.) My coffee tastes of cloves. My children taste of sleep. Televisions feed us Muzzy, the monster who speaks Spanish, and elephants who grieve in Africa. *This material is too disturbing for children.* A woman speaks of burning semen. The evangelist denies gay sex in the front seat, while his children listen in the back. The "homosexual lifestyle," my colleague assures me, involves brushing one's teeth in the morning.

--*Where'd the baby come from?* The stork. *What?* I adopted her.

--How poems end. We are accustomed to endings as conclusions, as what is or might be final. As the sum at the bottom of the receipt. As the dotted line. As an assertion of immortality. *My life a shambles, I turn to the beauty of nature.* (There's a boar in the next room, and he's about to conclude a root.) As a turn away, then toward. Try indecision, inconclusiveness, an opening into unawareness, a turn from the path to the freeway. My poem ends at rush hour. My poem adorns my bumper. My poem takes no ontological prisoners. My poem drives away at dark. My poem is an adviser to the president. My poem will be tried for war-crimes. My poem refuses closure, because it does not dare. My poem alludes to you. My poem is an SUV. My poem cannot overcome its fad. My poem is not to be found on this check. My poem just left the room. My poem is not appropriate to any audience. My poem appropriates audience. My poem is unaware of its affect. My poem comes in the mail, like Netflix. My poem goes out in the mail, like mortgage payments. My poem is a literal translation. My poem is in no language I can vouch for. My poem is a voucher that schools you. My poem is a back door woman. My poem will leave you.

--She says she's "homesick," and we believe her.

--The right-wing website puts "gay" in quotes.

--I have not yet mentioned the World Series. Nor yet the election. Nor yet the visiting poet whose gift was ambivalence.

--*LA Times:* The uncertainty surrounding the cause of death "complicates the grieving process," Turley said. "But the most important thing is my son served his country, and he's a casualty of war…. He was a beautiful person. He died way too young."

---She puts *humor* in quotes. Bush is not funny; he is a mass murderer. We must not laugh at him, for he is us, and we cannot laugh at ourselves. The court jester is so very 16th century. What we eat is poisoned, but we eat it anyway. The proposition is a preposition. Laugh with. Laugh at. Laugh off. All laughter canned. It runs past the expiration date; no more does laughter bring us health, like spinach. Popeye is an earnest man, if green. We hold these truths to be self-evident. Laughter is not a ladder, nor is it a leader. Laughter is happy to step out like a goose on the perfect German asphalt. We shall put L's on our clothing for "Laugher." I am the laugher. Does that sound flip to your ears? Then cut them off! The laughter club meets at the intersection of White and Devine each Tuesday at noon. Of its five members, three are gray-haired ladies. Admits she laughed at Bar. *George's father, Barbara*, quoth Borat.

--The untranslated word appears in italics. What is quoted is either fore- or backgrounded. We emphasize what we do not know. My daughter speaks to us in Japanese, sings her numbers in the tub, her colors at the table. *When is it best not to translate from one to another tongue?*

posted by Susan at 11:34 AM 0 comments

Saturday, November 11, 2006

--Houses are square, with pitched roofs. Trees have sturdy brown trunks, roofs of green. The ground is flat, a tight rope, and there is a round sun with feelers inside the house. Or there is a yellow sun in the ocean, where jellyfish and crabs are green. The girl has black hair and a design on her shirt. Sometimes there's a skateboard.

--He says he lied about Rumsfeld because it was the week of the election; he did not want it to turn on his decision. He says he lied so earnestly we know it's true. *But Cheney stays.*

--Her hair is cheese, and she wants to go home. The house is doing well, her neighbors say. The cards from her friends say, *I tried to call, but the phone was disconnected.*

--Where symbol is easy pattern and idiosyncrasy accident. Where pictures resemble other pictures. Where we find mediation, a seeing through that lacks illumination. The trunks are gray, the leaves uneven.

--He wrote "snowflakes." Anonymous, so there was no proof of authorship. Obsessed with the flow of information. What did the president know and when did he know it? And if he refuses to know, and if he does not?

--The land scars a lush brown in this rain. Mountains oscillate in cloud. He sees waterfalls, double rainbows, lizards, a baby toad in the shed. He sees what is there, when I look past. The shama thrush has a yellow belly, a white tail feather, sings loudest.

--When the poem's voice refuses to change. When the poem's voice is of statement only. I do this and I do that. Make things with words, but let them alter, give them a stream that takes mud and rocks with it. Make your poem a sluice, let it carry what is coal, irrigation water,

35

stolen water, the history of the land that's bent to moneyed purpose. The voice of the other: *nothing surprises me now; he wanted to make love on the altar,* says the escort of the priest.

--And then sometimes irony backfires like a cane truck. *She screamed at me for half an hour about the evils of development!*

--There is time to save him again, to take away that darkness, that crystal meth, that pleasure in candle-light. There is time to save us all, to rid us of all but our inhibitions, to replace them with what is rock solid, with what is true, with what the good lord knows will save us. Pity the man who knows so much.

--His poems' bitter nostalgia. The gate is gone, the boys are gone, the surfers are gone, the coke is gone, the girls are gone, the donkeys are gone, the beaches are (some of them) gone. Does the lyric ease or attenuate the poet's pain?

--Does he reflect "the indigenous voice"?

--What do you call the stand on which the dictionary sits?

--How do you spell "aloha," mommy?

--Does it become more or less clear why we write as we grow older? Are we widowed by earlier muses of lust and anger and anguish? Or do we re-marry them with reframed vows? *My wife is a very religious woman, one who takes her vows seriously. We've been married since 7 hours after we met. It's now 16 years. No, she didn't know.*

--He doesn't know what he'd do without celebrity. I watch the interview, having never heard his name before, curious how he deals with this fame I know nothing of.

--Madonna and Angelina let us speak of international adoption. Tom Cruise gives us leave to speak of theology. Arnold permits us politics.

--The snowflakes are up at Sears. The signs are in English and Spanish. Place colonized by snow and by language. L'homme avec le chewing gum. *It's the softer side of Sears.* Aloha no.

posted by Susan at 11:38 AM 1 comments

About Me

Name:Susan
Location:Kāne`ohe, Hawai`i

View my complete profile
Links

* Google News
* Edit-Me
* Edit-Me

Previous Posts

* November 19, 2006 --Nothing left except loss of ...
* November 12, 2006 --What I do not say to her: th...
* November 11, 2006 --Houses are square, with pitc...
* October 15, 2006 --No Imperial Mints in Chiswic...
* September 30, 2006 --The lyric in wartime. If...
* September 25, 2006 --The former President lost h...
* September 22, 2006 --The words bear weight, bu...
* September 21, 2006 --Encrusted object. Vessel...
* September 17, 2006 --The house. Read it as he...
* September 15, 2006 --Arrive at Lear, alone. W...

Powered by Blogger

Monday, October 16, 2006

--No Imperial Mints in Chiswick. Arc of empire turned down like
a collar against the gloom. Capital's the problem, as there's no
audience for Cambridge Marxists. The revolution started, but none
saw it behind the stone wall of Gonville & Caius. (Even the spelling
is capital.)

--*He made the hair on the back of my neck stand on end. I took one
look and wanted to say: you are not who you think you are; you are a
fraud. He had the worst body odor of anyone in England.* Keith said
it had to do with class.

--This is the church and this is the steeple. Open it up, and see all the
people.

--One of these poems moves from the inside out, and the other from
the inside in. Do you mean to say that only one of them appropriates?

--I surfed the bathroom floor for 20 seconds at least. And then
another one came.

--She kept breaking down. She said it was nerves, but each time
her voice broke she'd said the word "Iraq." We live in space but we
feel most deeply in our sound. The quaver of her voice altered our
positions in the room. We moved forward and then away, as if she
were the murderousness she decried. Dead from injuries sustained
when a roadside bomb exploded next to his convoy. We are told of
a place. But we are told in words. The sound of after-shock. *It's
coming again, I feel it.*

--Wallace Stevens is green on the book's front cover. The fuse that
drives the flower's cash.

--Compare physical to moral discomfort. Which figures the other?

--The congressman says Abu Ghraib was a "sex ring." The commentator says they were fraternity pranks. At least no one died, one said of the anti-pedophile pedophile's acts. Instant messaging makes a text of sex. *My master's eyes are nothing like this screen.*

--Three Americans sit face to face at a pub with three Brits. Two of the Brits and two of the Americans talk about 9/11 (11/9). So many more have died who have not been acknowledged, says Brit #2, a blonde. It's sheer manipulation of grief, says American #1 (bald), as #2 (dirty strawberry blonde) nods her head. American #3 (short cut brunette) falls silent. Brit #2 asks why. American #3 refuses to say. Minutes pass. Question rehearsed. American #3's voice breaks (see above, though it is not the same voice). She was on a bridge, saw the second plane turn. She cannot talk so casually. Not a question of content, but of degree. *Do not tell me what you feel, but where you feel, how you feel it.*

--She writes too much. He writes too little. She alludes too much to Plath, he to Petrarch. She's a witch, he's an arrogant prick. She's too obtuse, he's too clear. She's like O'Hara, he's like Oppen. Once named, allusion shuts down its line. He got the one about the world to stand on.

posted by Susan at 1:01 AM 3 comments

Saturday, September 30, 2006

--The lyric in wartime. If stealth bombers are honu, what are the honu? If surf sounds like artillery fire, then how is artillery defined? If there is beauty in war, war is still not "natural." If the point is that we cannot not see the war before us, then how to reconcile (that's not the word) beauty with disgust? *There is one attack every 15 minutes against Americans in Iraq. Polls indicate that 60 percent of Iraqis favor attacks against Americans.*

--I have not translated the word honu.

--She looks wonderful; she had her hair done, I'm told. Friendly and talkative. *I'm still looking for a ride home,* she tells me. Our conversation a constant diversion away, and then again, *it's hard to get anything done here.*

--The chair of the committee that protects children from sexual predators on the internet was himself a sexual predator on the internet. *We're secret agents*, Sangha says.

--When he was confronted with the failure of his policies, the defense secretary said *you wage war with the army that you've got.*

--The green trees blaze in yellow light, the purple clouds. Frog song cedes to dove song.

--*He was just shot*, says the contractor in the video, of his colleague. We are shown a steering wheel. No one to drive the car. School principal killed by student. Two 13 year olds arrested for arson in Wai`anae. The sexual predator had a list of the girls' names. He took his hostages, killed one before turning the gun on himself. This is how our fairy tales end.

--When should we refuse translation? When is the refusal to translate unethical?

--*These are terrorists who want to kill Americans. They are the lowest of the low; they are scum.* All evidence collected by a) water boarding (picture of a table and a bucket at Tuol Sleng); or b) sleep deprivation (photo of a stereo system), shall be used against them. The president is arbiter of this, as all things. He is not a man who uses vague expressions, like "inhumanity" or "human degradation."

--Angelina Jolie looks pregnant again.

--The Critic arrives, armed with a quiver of Judgments, and wrestles my language to the floor. She says the author speaks from a position of privilege, one that blinds her to realities that cannot be contained in lyric or in ironic poems. Irony saves the Poet from 1) the horror and 2) any beliefs that might mitigate 1), which she does not recognize but intuits. Note that "intuition" is an issue to be raised at a later time.

--The insurgent must be put in prison.

--The insurgent hates Americans.

--The insurgent will be dealt to a third country, which has fewer qualms.

--The critic must practice crying. She must talk on a subject about which she is especially arch, but she must deliver her words in such a way that she cries. She will be denied access to kleenexes or handkerchiefs, and will have no right to leave her podium. The critic may not employ artificial substances in her efforts to cry. She must rely on her own emotions, her own physiology. She must do this before an audience of at least two dozen of her colleagues, those who least expect her to react in this way.

--At Jesus camp, children cry. They pray for the President, and they pray to become warriors for the Lord. At Jesus camp, the children speak in tongues, they dance, and they repeat what their spiritual leader says. At Jesus camp, the children learn to be parallel insurgents. At Jesus camp, other cheeks are not turned, except toward the echo of gunfire. Jesus also wandered the desert.

--I envy the lyric poet. The lyric poet still sees the sunrise, still marvels at the thrush in the doorway, still calls out the names of artists. The lyric poet sees through perversity, knows the true forces are natural ones. She knows Bush is not the sun, Rumsfeld is not the moon, and Cheney is not the tide.

posted by Susan at 11:11 AM 1 comments

Monday, September 25, 2006

--*The former President lost his temper*. Loss of content in our public life. Only forms remain, intonation, affect. *Why did you yell in my mom's house?* Radhika asks our neighbor.

--*She sounded like she does when her hands shake*. She does not want to be there. Bryant calls to ask about her things. A tape on osteoperosis. No. Foundations of Economics (from the 1930s). No. The Soviet shelf. No. The Nazi shelf. No. The Greeks, the Moslems. No. The speech and drama shelf. No. Encyclopedias, no. Check registers back to 1964. No. Harry Truman, no. Mrs. Ike, no.

--*Was her reading too intense?*

--Grief is excess of sound. Anger is excess of form. Sadness can lack, or still exceed. Excess is overtone, the note beyond the note you sound. Without the tone, there is no object. *Did I kill Bin Laden? No. But I tried.*

--My task is to inventory sentences, place them in order, box them up and ship them in a container. They are a sturdy furniture, haphazard art. They are boxes of papers, bills, pieces of a dissertation. A computer shopper magazine (discard). Titles whose aura was a life, or two, or three. The house is now full of light. A girl wanders through the rooms, trying keys at the windows. My mother knows none of this.

--My father might be in the garden, or the scarecrow that wears his hat. Let him wander the house this last, inspect the plumbing, lights, air conditioning, the rows of beans, sort through medals, papers, release them as excess.

posted by Susan at 12:44 PM 0 comments

Friday, September 22, 2006

--The words bear weight, but they are light! Apish, accidia. Push outward, against. *They will be tried with "evidence" they know nothing of. They will be interrogated with "methods" approved by the commander and what they say will be held against them.* This is "compromise."

--*We do not compromise our beliefs* is a phrase that is now "inoperative."

--How does The Torture Bill make you feel? Ted Koppel asks the Dalai Lama if he and the pope like each other.

--A young couple, speaking Spanish, went to pick up a bed and a desk. A neighbor went to see mom, who was "pleasant."

--If it no longer matters if we repeat the words, mark them with quotations, italicize them, hurl abuse at them, stencil them on sidewalks and tread on them, obstruct them with typos, yell "halt" at any who read them too quickly, offer extra credit to students to vote in the primary ("what's a primary?"). What shall be the form of our resistance? How do we spell "defence"?

--BONE. GOES. MULE. CLOSE. THOSE. THESE. I got it right!

--The words bear weight, but they are light! Where first shall we turn the light? (I'm offered "fireplace" for "first.")

--Irony. The I ron ron, the I ron ron. Irritant. Party of opposition in name only. No words. They lose, and yet they fear losing again. Define "loss."

--She is in a cottage that floats. I hear a dog bark. It's a large dog, she says, St. Bernard in the mix. She has her father's ashes. He was last well (*I hate your use of the word "illness"*) in Canada, and now he's back. She thinks he's better now. Ashes in her backpack. We can at least work on the dead, recover them for happiness.

posted by Susan at 1:03 PM 0 comments

Thursday, September 21, 2006

--Encrusted object. Vessel emptied, by chair and by bed. Emissaries. Movers, shifters. A house holds its objects as a sentence does its punctuation. Where there is sentiment, install a comma, semi-colon, period. *I have to remind him at the end of every sentence to add a period, or he simply doesn't do it.* Attention distilled, distracted. Where there is only object, dash.

--Write a fast poem and a slow one. Then switch.

--He will be last of us to sleep there. *Take the pokers, the carpet, the rocking chair. The painting upstairs, the beds, the sofa, the wrought iron chairs and table.* Consumer chronicle. We refuse the spell because we know they're trying to sell us something. Alliteration fails any more to seduce. The car in the meadow is not a Romantic poet, contemplating the language of cloud and tree whisper. The lawn is not a meadow. The sounds of grasshoppers have been exhumed, but not yet reassembled. Suburb is imitation, mimicry, artifice.

--The form is sturdy, "well built." No broken tower, gravel cascade. She planned the house herself, its fixtures, appliances, the wallpaper. The form was convention, but it was chosen by her. I will leave blanks in the lines for you to fill in. In the suburbs we do not leave our comfort zone. One neighbor tried twice to kill himself. The second time he "succeeded."

--*The USA is more nuts than I am.*

--CIA agents refused to interrogate prisoners in the secret prisons, for fear they'd be prosecuted. A "compromise" is due on the torture bill. Bush says Geneva Convention language is "too vague." Sangha writes his spelling words three times a week.

--According to Neruda, poets are like bakers. They are not "mini-gods." Your responsibility is to the family recipe. No solitude is insurmountable. None is to be desired, except in shifts. *I promised myself I would never in my life vote.*

--When a neighbor went to see her, she was in the beauty shop. She wonders whom to hire to get her home. She wonders why Joe hasn't called; he was 12 years older. She has made no friends, because the people there are all old. She keeps our photos in the drawer because otherwise she's too homesick. They walked around the garden, stopped in the gazebo. She looked good.

--*The coup has already happened.*

posted by Susan at 1:50 PM 0 comments

Sunday, September 17, 2006

--The house. Read it as her autobiography: dark wood, crumbling wallpaper (dark again, checked squares of brown and white), the paintings (representational, a mill in the woods, some storm-tossed ships), the 1970s style modified shag carpet, parquet floors (dark), fireplaces (three of them), front and back yards needing to be mown. How did she come to this?

--*They're just silly stories. No one's interested in them.*

--The "home." Read it as biography. A porch outside the Country Lane, picnic bench, umbrella, a brightness next to the window. Outside inside. Remember your corridor by the decor. The artifice must present nature, or a loving intervention in it. What you remember shall comfort you and what you do not is simply not here. This sanctuary is not only for birds.

--She calls from the woods. The campsites will close soon for the season. I think I hear a fire. She wants a "practical brain" to speak to her brain.

--House and woods are forms of privacy. They enclose, though in altered perspective. There is limit there. What else is shelter but limit that is not confinement? Confinement is not birth but swaddling, smothering, folding in. Kick them off, write in private for a while. Yet this is part of it, this writing and then posting, bill on a virtual tree, most wanted stretch of text located by accident, or referral. This is about the problem of what is private and what public, what ought not be shared and what must be. The process is not fiction, but enactment. Easement. When the property is sold, it can no longer be taken as the story of her life, or of mine. Interpolated, perhaps. But the quotes have gone missing.

--They are building trenches around Baghdad to keep insurgents out. It is the job of an insurgent to surge in, to enter the inner, to exit nothing but where he was, which was hidden. Dozens of bodies were found this week inside the city's imagined moats. Sectarian violence, it's called. Test questions: how would you wall in a sect, while walling out an insurgent? How would you do so in as few steps as possible? How would you describe the geometrical shape required?

--Define "out."

--Define "sect."

--Define "wall."

--There is an offer on her house, for it "as is." The closed house is yours. The open one will not be.

posted by Susan at 1:19 PM 0 comments

Friday, September 15, 2006

--Arrive at Lear, alone. Were I Lear's Rove, I'd counsel the politics of despair. *They want to kill your families,* the president tells a reporter, hand on his arm, protectively. There is no moisture on the glass, nothing but feeling that grows so large it cannot fit the community pool. It is too large to drown. He left pictures of himself cradling a black gun, staring down its sights at us, involuntary onlookers. We do not choose to read. Texts are imposed upon us. Miss Swiss is a steamboat whose captain is named Steve. The story ends with a good smell, clams baked on her deck. Osama is a bad man. The president wants him dead or alive, but he is neither. He is an image that comes back and back.

--She's been moved to a place that is much the same. Country Lane #11. The people are kind, the food is good, she wants a ride home. *It's a home for old folks, and I don't want to spend the rest of my life here.* Her house will be shown this weekend.

--This week's spelling words include "shake," "went," "scratch" (for bonus points), and "every." You must write each word three times, alphabetize the list, write them again on the back of a small piece of paper, then take your test. *The librarian says he's not interested in anything,* the teacher reports.

--Better the sins of empathy than its lack. Key words in this text include: "privilege," "gender," "race," "institutions," "narcissism." "Empathy" must not elide any of these terms, for fear of their erasure. I must feel empathy only for my kind, lest I bend categories, ignore my privilege. If emotion is itself a privilege (what hungry person has time for it?), then interrogate it. Critique, intellect, idiolect, locution, execution. The seven Chinese brothers were a perfect Adam Smith machine. One did the seeing, another the hearing, a third the crying, and the others were strong. When in doubt, drown your enemies in tears.

--A panda sat in the back garden under an umbrella. He told the story of his uncle, a poor panda, whose modest house was invaded by a robber raccoon. "Welcome!" he cried, trying hard to remember what he could share with the robber, who was so obviously in need. "Here, take my coat," the panda said to the raccoon. "It's thin and torn, but it will cover you when it gets cold." The raccoon fled, thinking the panda mad. In the last frame, the panda sits atop a mountain, wondering after the raccoon.

--Discuss the role of empathy in the story, above. Does the panda's empathy hurt him? What do you think will be the effect of the panda's empathy on the raccoon? Where will the panda get his next coat? What is the relationship between pragmatism and feeling in this story? Can feeling be pragmatic, or is it always in excess of sense? Is sense a natural term, or has it been imposed by cultural norms? Would the panda feel different were he a mouse? What if the raccoon were a wolf? Where is grandma in all this? The red frock?

--The interrogator wonders which rule to follow, the rule of law or that of conscience, of cold type or of empathy, wherever that lives. He says experiments are not "close to home," but Ted Kooser is. After you spell that word, define it. "What's an execution?" Sangha asks. The enemy might adjust to our techniques. Water-boarding, surf-boarding.

--She stopped the car in her driveway. She called out to the white bird to come. He came to her, and stayed for years.

posted by Susan at 12:42 PM 0 comments

Sunday, September 10, 2006

(yesterday was the 9th, not the 8th)

--*Ultimately, it's just leaves and wind.* Ultimately is an awfully big word. There's also tomorrow. Where will you be tomorrow? *I don't know, but I'll see it.*

--When abstraction is evasion and incision, apt invasion.

--Abstraction is the word "it." It transcends. It takes leaves and wind and removes them from the senses, reduces them to grammar. "It's just leaves and wind" is a sentence; it's like leaves in wind, but it's not those leaves in that wind. *Feelings of detachment and estrangement from others.*

--"It transcends all that." It = an entire complex, "seeing feelingly," though blind. That = the cure, imagined to reduce seeing and feeling to their lowest common denominators. The "it" works against the "that," because "that" is thought to be the enemy of "it." "It," a skinnier word, more easily spoken, defeats "that" in a late round TKO, after several rounds go to "that" on one referee's card.

--When asked what poet they hate, most say without hesitation, "Shakespeare."

--If I were to write one of those sonnets that persuades, the first quatrain would be about sickness, freewheeling thoughts, the shaking Shakespearean body; the second would add figures to this proposition, autumn leaves, the wind, the coming chill, despite the body's early summer harvest; the third would suggest an interlocutor, someone to remark on sad eyes, or how the levee's gonna break. The couplet, as it must, would suggest a companion, one who rhymes reason and then seals it with a stop.

--The haiku version posits the wind, the leaves, announces the bellicosity of frog. The glint of a white eye's eye. The cloud's break against the blue. The blues, but Japanese.

--The macaronic reads: don't! Desperate ontologies natter, apostrophe travels. Exclamation! That's my point.

--The insult poem is a weekend hunter in the woods. He's lost his porto-potty and his camouflaged paper. He's a desperate man. He sprays the woods with several rounds, then retires to drink beside the fire.

--My mother may be moved, again. Google earth reveals a campus surrounded by more space to walk, to meditate, to consider the abstractions dementia brings. Those few thoughts repeated, like a refrain that can't.

--I want the word "dovetail," but I cannot see it mean.

posted by Susan at 11:56 AM 0 comments

Saturday, September 09, 2006

1. September Eight

--Rides, car, home, keys, solitude, mother, no meds, no occupational therapy, no no no. Mom bleeds into A., and they are both my daughters.

--*Signs and symptoms of post-traumatic stress disorder typically appear within three months of the traumatic event. However, in some instances, they may not occur until years after the event.* Define "event," as if discrete. Define event in such a way it lives. Is horror, not event. Freddy Krueger without delighted screams. Trauma in repetition, like constant Wagner. The event is a ghost of itself, and the man with brown hair reappears in dreams. There are pills for anxiety, for insomnia, for nightmares, for bipolar disorder, but there is none for family. There are ghosts within the ghosts, the cribs, the rooms you move to to avoid him, there are ghosts within him you cannot reach, and there are ghosts she would deny you see, because of course there are no ghosts.

--Bryant saw a ghost, and checked his watch to see what time it was. There are warriors who march through your house if you build it in the wrong spot. There are warriors who will tell you how to get home if you are hurt. There are ghosts who are horny, ghosts who love and ghosts who kill. There was a ghost outside by the pickup truck.

--You must perform well, make demands, have a strong voice. You feel like shit, you smell like shit, you are shit for now, but the squeaky wheel. Act. Trippingly, and all that. Stand up, so the diaphragm can push the air. Hamlet played himself, at least. You are not Ophelia. You must survive your own script. Pick up the comedies, for god's sake.

posted by Susan at 7:30 PM 0 comments

2. September Eight

--How non-violent people become violent. *I will either take off somewhere in my mind or commit homicide.* He calls the house. She calls me. I call two other women. One of the women calls the crisis center. Spends all night, which is her day, walking her there. When I ask the man if I've reached detox, he says, "I can neither confirm nor deny that." I call her mother. Her mother calls me. *I wanted you to know I'm on her side.*

--They're family men. They didn't mean to kill (stomped his head into the sidewalk, such a sound). My brother never would have done such a thing. My husband. My father. Testimony's burden: fact framed by need.

--How violent people turn non-. Empathy's bad name, feeling with a feeling as—the man who wrote holocaust testimony because his childhood was bad—congruence, shift in the tide between here and there marked not as transition but as exact same. Our larger politics demands reason! By one and by one we lose our focus. Not Marcel's cobblestones, but Hitler's. *A failed painter wrote a book,* the president says. And now they make videos.

--My empathy is memory, is a container into which her experience sometimes fits, shallow grave or swimming pool (death by water), though mine is a memory of overpasses. Not to pass over, but under by way of air. The air is human. I am the limbless woman.

--Risk factors include (these are bullet points) a previous history of depression or other emotional disorder; a previous history of physical or sexual abuse; a family history of anxiety; early separation from parents; being part of a dysfunctional family; alcohol abuse; drug abuse.

--Casualties are down in Iraq because victims of car bombs are no longer counted in the statistics. If you die the wrong way, you will not be counted.

--She drives in her car, dreaming of Lebanon. She pays for gas, feels bombs in that other air, which is also hers. The disease is not empathy; empathy is symptom, side-effect, erosion, self-wound rendered in another tongue. *Her mother is not capable.* I call her mother, say they do not know where she is.

--I told my mother to stay away, called a friend. We drove to a lake, walked in the woods with her daughter. Presence is not empathy; it's better.

--What we owe to those who consider suicide: words, a prayer, presence, gratitude for the offer of an Ozzie Smith card, network, time (in whatever space), patience, platitude.

posted by Susan at 11:51 AM 0 comments

Thursday, September 07, 2006

--The dove walks two steps, then falls, walks another, settles on its side, walks, turns over down the hill. It covers ground, but allegorically. Hours in, I consider releasing the cat, then refuse him exit.

--Mom complains the hospital had too many old people in it. *They (we) were not in good shape.* She's fine, don't worry. She'll be working on a ride home. *Perhaps you'll come someday and take me away.*

--Bryant orders me more memory for my birthday. *It might be nice to lose one's memory,* she said yesterday. *I want you out of my refrain.* (Dylan)

--Radhika and Sangha wonder if mom was in a wheelchair at the hospital. *I know, I know what grandma Wawa is saying,* Sangha says, his arms waving. *No, no, no, I can walk!*

--She called last night to ask that someone have her locks changed. She doesn't want us to worry when she goes away this weekend.

-- The bird in survival mode, the book I try to read (a man studies scripture to confront a quack teacher), the kids in school, trees filling with wind (my computer wants to add "shield"), orange cat asleep on the tiles.

11:00 Crossword and Name That Song;

1:00 Jane Addams Born

2:00 Ball Toss

3:00 Grandma Moses Born

4:00 Bingo / Documentary

5:45 Wheel of Fortune

Her undergraduate thesis was on Jane Addams. Hull House. My mother has always hated games.

--Is fortune a wheel or is there a more precise geometry? What has the Buddhist wheel to do with Vanna White? What do we do with vowels, once we buy them?

--Sangha copies his spelling words, puts them in alphabetical order. He memorizes books, then "reads" them back. He studies the clues, the pictures, the first letters, the sense of the story. His first 100 words are on flashcards. Or, and, then, word. The hard ones are which, what, when. He replaces them with how.

--Miriam conflates Lissa and Lucia, writes Larissa. Healer and sufferer, each in their turn.

posted by Susan at 4:22 PM 0 comments

Wednesday, September 06, 2006

--There's responsibility in language because we assume an
interlocutor when we speak (Levinas, reported by Leonard). I
say: I've been there. I say: you will not get help unless [she calls,
sounds more clear, we chat about music, DiFranco and Dylan, each
according to her generation. 1997 was in a good era, she says, before
Mother Teresa died.]

--I say you are my interlocutor. I say you must take care. I say you
need an advocate. *Advocate, advocate, advocate.* You say there is
none. I say one might appear. I say you must take care first, before
you leave. There's noise and music on the porch; you turn down the
sound, up the volume. You say there are locks to be changed there. I
say stay there (a different there); let someone else attend to locks.

--You are my interlocutor because I say so. Some evenings
meanings stray out beyond the lake, the ducks, the policemen, the
systematizers, the stardust, the genes spliced against your will, the
mother who is so kind, the degradation, the songs. Then you are not,
but I speak in any case, or sit with the phone, as if it were a baby, up
at 4 a.m. as you say you were. I've taken her out of her cradle, away
from the power, and just after she beeps, she sleeps.

--Combinations are what open them. *You know how hard transitions
are,* says Mr. Ellis. *The kids have to go to their desks, then get down
on the floor, then wander around the room, then do their math.* It's
these combinations confuse us, not that confusion's a bad thing, but
you have to get to know it, make friends with it, accept that it will
not be by your side for long, may strike out for the lake, or the pier,
or be borne upon the bier, where death gives life because we insist
it must, and the shed door opens and the bikes appear. A man on a
bike in Wai`anae was beaten to death by three men after a traffic
altercation. *Always had a smile on his face. I think he was homeless.
Sometimes a girlfriend on the back of the bike, and he'd wave.*
Where's the life in that?

--The poet's arrogance promises eternal value. He's a snake oil salesman, meaning to offer eternal life for current reproduction. My students wonder why he wants this. "His love for the young man was idealized, not lust," one adds.

--She says she's said too much.

--The way poets love others for what they bring to their poems, I say. There's an economy of supply and demand, though it does not exist within capitals.

--Mom was in the ER last night: difficulties breathing, several broken ribs. She could not remember anything. I called, became her memory. She has not lost hers; it's been given to me to hold. So much have I forgotten that now I cannot call back. The corrupted file is beyond salvage, and autocorrect, while it's turned itself on, cannot replace the word dust, stories burned beyond recognition, then scattered at the beach.

--It's ritual, this mother daughter forgetting. What she remembers of me is now her. And what I remember of her is now fact: she fell on a sprinkler and later complained of pains in her side. That is all I know.

--She and she bear no responsibilities in this exchange. It is I who must parse my words, take care not to say what truth shall maul (the lion's paws are sharp), and it is I who must remember, in order to sort the useful from what can be used against. A human shield. The bomber kills self before others. So the self must be held hostage to our care.

--Put others before yourself. Antidote to violence, or time trickery. I say "good morning," or wherever you are in time. She talks "time-space," when I mean, "it's afternoon where you are." The leaps are pre-made, like poems. You simply mis-see them, plug them into the wrong equation, get an answer that will only suffice at a later time, space.

--I'm here only when they need someone to take over. No one else is here. I know nothing of your mother. Perhaps you can call someone else. I know this is not what you want to hear.

--I'll call back later.

posted by Susan at 3:31 PM 0 comments

Monday, September 04, 2006

--One of the little people was held hostage. Outside the "home," a crowd of dwarves and midgets screamed their anger at the hostage taker, midget on the roof (no fiddle). Voices pitched high, like the music. We knew it was a parable, because everyone was small. We knew the institution stood in for the State, because everyone who was small spoke German. And the film was in black and white.

--She holds herself hostage by a lake. This is not a parable, though it might read as one, given she has escaped the institution and repeats a phrase from Eliot. If it is a parable, I want her to read less literally. Consider that there are four levels, at least, that this is hell's level, allegory's basement knee deep in water you dream your eyeballs see from below. If you rise too quickly, you get the exegetical bends, but if you refuse, no one sees the beauty of molecules meeting stardust, not in the key of A. I don't ask for the fork that spears as it measures sound, but [the sound of a child's song] abstraction's anchor against what pulls us away, like the tides. There may be a level that does not combine sorrow with joy, gives us sorrow pure, no engines to give it flight/fright. And another. Pass through in your orb of glass, my detective of mixed-states, render yourself clear of this genetic mimesis, mini-series. Reading follows a bad compass, if magnets warp, and they do. Genes need not follow straight paths; they too are queer.

--The literature of boundaries and frontiers depends on there being boundaries and frontiers. If they melt, there are no words to describe crazy canons of Spanglish, or Pidgin, or Midwest accents, the broadness of their vowels as they migrate. It may be called the Peace Bridge, but it requires two shores to declare itself.

--The form of this madness is an amoeba, altering with each response. It is not dementia, the fixed muscle of a single thought. Or it is a man-of-war that stings itself. We know thy sting, refuse it. Save your coupons; you may need them later. But for now, the tank is full, the roads are clear, the clock's got a fresh battery. No acid spills, but a windshield of clear skies and sails dots the lake like bad punctuation, lovely though they spoil our simple sentences.

--We who have attended to that edge know its sharpness, its necessity. Let it be your bodhissatva, turning the boat over until only what is good remains. In your frail bark find a shore, build a fire, sniff the needles. They also pine.

posted by Susan at 12:35 AM 0 comments

Sunday, September 03, 2006

--The form is our death, or I should say, our death is a form. I mean to elide form into style, the style of our being conjoined with the form that describes us, and our going. I read her life, her dying, as a form or style, which is my appropriation. There is never propriety in our appropriation, though property shall come of it. Her style is refusal: refusal to change, to reconsider, to respond, to renovate. There is constancy in her decline. He writes about his use of "normalcy" to describe a government, a literal state. She claims her normalcy as ours, and who is to say no to that? I ask my students to pronounce "content" in the first sonnet. Which syllable bears the strain that calls it noun or verb? *He cannot let himself die,* he said, *because he's too afraid to face himself.* Odd myth, death as accounting, the final checkbook entry that reads "food!" or other item. She would say she was "practical," not "creative," that she should have been an accountant, not an actress as she briefly was. The ledger is a reading back on our qualities, those we invent as descriptions of our habits, once they accrue. They are the form we make to hold ourselves. Hers was brick, and it never changed.

--*It's been raining a lot here.* Weather as disruption of certainty, ceasura between certitudes.

--83% of my battery remains. I could write a poem based on the time is takes to run the battery down to zero. But a battery can—usually—be revived.

--Iraqi civilian deaths have jumped upward. There is or is not a civil war in Iraq. Were there a civil war, our "tactics" would change. The emphasis is on us. Four soldiers who killed civilians will be tried. He said he felt threatened. The woman he raped was doubtless a danger, especially when he shot her in the face. The word "civil" does not govern here. It is the form of our war that worries us, but its content is blood on the street.

--Expect more Al-Qaeda tapes before the mid-term elections. More war drums against Iran. More Nazi metaphors. "This is not politics."

--Radhika draws and draws, a pile of paintings for her sister in Miami. What names do we have for this family: two sisters, three mothers, one brother to one sister, (and then another), and a father to sister and brother? (I forget a father, a mother.) *Nuclear* will not do.

posted by Susan at 11:19 AM 0 comments

Saturday, September 02, 2006

--*"I'm still trying to get a ride home, but it's hard to do." "What else are you doing there?" "Oh we play games and have activities. I'm really quite bored."*

--A summer student calls unexpectedly. *Do you believe our natural state is apathy?* she asks. *You wrote that in a poem. Do you tell your students what you believe?*

--*Promise that you'll read my work not as a professor but as a human being.*

--Sangha's teacher looks at me and says, "I wonder if he just doesn't get it. He gets this blank look on his face when I tell him things. I can't find a place in the room where he won't be distracted."

--My student defines poetry as *what makes the ordinary extraordinary.* The suburb is a maze too easily solved. But there is something in it that houses our fear of abstraction in plain landscape, its frame of solid wood. The man I hailed at the airport three weeks ago is dead--so many forms of his verb conjugated in so few days. I am trying to fit him into a small house, to protect him with the poverty of memory, to keep him in the smallest room, where no evidence of him can leak out. I am afraid of his death. It is too ordinary to hold in my hand like a firefly, or a cat's chin. To conjugate is to change; the end is signaled by the verb that fails to find its exit. I ask that his end with we.

posted by Susan at 4:41 PM 0 comments
About Me

Name:Susan

View my complete profile
Links

* Google News
* Edit-Me
* Edit-Me

Previous Posts

* September 30, 2006 --The lyric in wartime. If...
* September 25, 2006 --The former President lost h...
* September 22, 2006 --The words bear weight, bu...
* September 21, 2006 --Encrusted object. Vessel...
* September 17, 2006 --The house. Read it as he...
* September 15, 2006 --Arrive at Lear, alone. W...
* September 10, 2006 (yesterday, the 9th, not 8th) ...
* September Eight --Rides, car, home, keys, soli...
* September 8, 2006 --How non-violent people bec...

Thursday, August 31, 2006

--*She looks good, calm, friendly; they're not giving her much Ativan,*
Karen reports. *She still prefers sleeping in the buff. They have to
remind her to get dressed in the morning.*

--Sangha brings home his Cub Scout bandanna, shows me how to
slip it through the metal slide. He takes his scout handbook to bed or
I could look at the badges he already wants to earn. I open the book
this morning to its first section, *Child Abuse.* What to do when a
little old lady offers to walk your younger sister home. Bruce Weigl's
scoutmaster, his drunken breath in little Bruce's sleepy face.

--A man wearing a teeshirt with Arabic script on it is kept off a plane.
*Was he an innocent traveler, or was he trying to make a political
statement?* (This really happened.)

--She has the family pictures, neatly folded, in her baggage, ready to
take them home. She doesn't ask Karen for a ride, but hopes to see
her at home next time.

--If you oppose the Iraq war, or favor a scheduled pull-out, you are
an *appeaser* in the mold of Neville Chamberlain. If you oppose
the Iraq war, you are *morally confused.* If you do not see the good
that's happened in New Orleans, you are a *pessimist.* If you are
a pessimist, you cannot fathom the *progress* that's being made. If
you do not see that our *enemies are Islamo-fascists*, you do not
understand the world we are living in. If you believe that Bush broke
the law, you consider yourself above it. If you do not see that Israel
won its war. If you do not see that paying taxes is a sacrifice for the
republic. If you do not see that democracy is beginning to flourish.

--That was a poem only in the sense that its meaning is not apparent.
We look for meanings below the surfaces of these words we do not
understand. While meaning is not apparent, notice how each sentence

"makes sense." It's what happens between the sentences that trips us up, teases us into sense (or non-), if we only pause to notice. We must take time to read our poems. We must look up words like *fascist.* Like *Chamberlain.* Like *democracy.*

--I am reading a dissertation. One of its narrators has dementia, but she is proud of it. She speaks strangely well, but the world she describes is not aware of its edges. *That was the one thing in all the reading I understood,* he says. Meaning lives in limitation, though it wanders like an old woman in a home, for whom the doors are open (unless it's hot), who walks the grounds as she pleases, unaware of the chain link fence, painted green to match the forest (beside the highway that stitches this suburb to its metropolis). If it slips through the chain's link, this permeable edge, it's gone. But it may show up elsewhere, tagged for identification. The bar code still shows.

--She asks me the difference between *eulogy* and *elegy.*

--We used to write elegies for the dead, and they became stars in our firmament. I write of my mother in her dying, not past it. *The prepositions are always the hardest.* These words are for her, through you. The poem is a vessel of blood.

posted by Susan at 2:51 PM 0 comments

Wednesday, August 30, 2006

--*Form follows dysfunction.* (Lennard J. Davis)

--We changed the form to say Radhika's first language was English, so she won't *be tracked for years* as a second-language speaker. Radhika: rabbit. *She's the best in her class,* sensei says.

--If I am her second mother, then I gave her a second mother tongue. My first mother takes herself away from me, word by mother-word. Not anaphora but aphasia, not amanuensis but amnesia, not piscatory but piss, not copasetic but coping, not lexicon but laxative. These last are "in" her future, small container of remnant metaphor. *When the jar fills up with jelly beans, then we'll have a party.*

--None of my students looked up the word *vitaver,* save one. *Essential oil,* she muttered.

--It's a poem about death, I volunteer. Jenn reads *museums* as *mausoleums.* The transcriber edits out Bush's *ums,* as if he failed to stutter between episodes of failed grammar.

--The sentences make sense, I tell them. It's what happens between them that does not. My mother's sentences work. *I am in Afghanistan and I need to get a train to Wooster, Ohio* has a subject (though we wonder who's represented by the *I*). She is in a named place (Afghanistan, though she has never, to our knowledge, been there). This subject has desires (*I need to*). She recognizes the grammar of transport.

--Who placed a jar in Tennessee again?

--A Vietnam poet breaks down over the term *vis-à -vis*. Rumsfeld calls some among us *appeasers*. CNN asks if we think *fascism* is an appropriate term (let alone *Islamo-*). Bush is reading Hamlet; Dowd points out that someone drowned. The bodies are in the water, on the ground, the bodies are cord wood. We will smoke the words out of their caves. *You can make old words new,* says Horace. *Just invent new ones, using the Greek.* I realize in mid-sentence what I mean to say, hesitate, consider self-censorship and then blurt, *so invent new ones, using Arabic.*

--We can call her *demented,* though that is not who she is. I can say she has identities, but not one that governs her tongue. I can say she is still my mother, but cannot say how she bore me, because my amnesia preceded me as hers will follow her. She wanders like a wireless link, room to room, dusk to deeper dusk. The musk of the old folds over her, like a mask she cannot see for wearing it. Out is the word we think of next. Out of her mind, if not ours. Out of sight. Out of it. Off-line.

posted by Susan at 5:34 PM 0 comments

Sunday, August 27, 2006

--Yesterday we could call out, but our voices broke up on the other end. Bryant kept muttering about *outgoing packets.* The cable guys understood.

--*I'm not doing well,* Mom said this morning. *I'm trying to get a ride but it's hard to get anything done here. I'm homesick.* "How are you otherwise?" *I eat a lot.* By the time Bryant gets the phone, passed him by Sangha, she says *I love you, sweetie,* and hangs up.

--The Box is full of checks, bank statements, stray insurance statements, Mastercard bills, treasury statements, Medicare reports, everything that was swept off the dining room table. The Box, despite its scatter, contains episodes of order; checkbooks neatly kept, years of bank statements in chronological order (though I suspect the neighbor did some of this). 2002-2004, organized. Then the scatter starts. The archivist, if there is one, is out to lunch. The last checkbook: she recorded checks, then pasted returned ones beside the stubs. Most checks match their stubs, though some are off by two or three numbers. And then the last two pages. There's a check to Susan Schultz, one to Susan S. Webster, another to Susan Webster. $120.00. *For food!* scribbled on the stub.

--Poems must make sense, must communicate, my student writes in response to Ashbery, who, it seems, does not. This my poem, my blog, my sad report, makes sense (emphasis on the making, not the sense); its sentences push forward (which is back); they contain thoughts (like ships), and you, my readers, understand (or so you say). I write because I do not understand. Writing fails to make it mean. Where communication fails to make mean what cannot be made sense of, what then? *Mystery and death, the way you like it.*

--The meaning I make is all excess. It is the suburb of my white flight, my fear, my bastion of meaning otherwise. It is not wise, but it will do (doing is necessary to making, and meaning comes of that). I will make of my well cut lawn and my back fence an artifice to order. Altar. The banality of the Alzheimer's home only mirrors this. Where art is management and what is managed eludes capture, like the rabbits my father gamed with for years in his garden. Managed care as the art of instituting *home*. Assisted care living is a step above the nursing home. Home is where you do not want to be.

--And yet you miss some version of it. I wonder can she still see it, or are there only beads of words—names of the missing—to lure her there. Dementia as self-kidnap. The girl was in a cellar for eight years. It was prison and it was home. My mother wishes to return to where there was a home. But it was broken then.

--Poetry is language that calls attention to itself. Our sight words for today are:

home

broken

meaning

Box

making

checks

It is especially important that you know sight words that do not sound as they are spelled. *Sight* is one of these, as is *know.*

posted by Susan at 12:04 PM 0 comments

Friday, August 25, 2006

--*We want the mind to last,* Leonard writes, remembering his grandmothers. *We want the mind to last.*

--Once they fall, the strawberry guavas Sangha and Radhika pick to eat (*I want dark red!*) stink sweet, crushed on the sidewalk by our school-bound feet.

--*She's doing beautifully,* the director tells me. *I was told she's a loner, but she's making friends, doing activities; just today she went on a trip.*

--I wonder whom to believe, the woman who wants a cab to take her home to Ohio, or the woman who tells me the cab will not be needed. *She gets herself to meals.* The word is *functional.*

--*May I go by myself?* Radhika says, once we arrive at school.

--She had a story about the bay of Naples. One day she so craved solitude she rented a rowboat and she rowed that little boat to the middle of the bay. Looking up, she saw a soldier friend rowing out to meet her in another boat, gesturing wildly in the air. *I didn't think you'd want to be alone,* he said.

--*Is this what it means to be a grown-up?* Miriam asks. This must be the question we were not asked as children. *What will you be when you grow up?* Caregiver in absentia, daughter over distances. *It wouldn't be easier if you moved across the street,* my cousin said.

posted by Susan at 5:08 PM 0 comments

Thursday, August 24, 2006

--She's fine, she's fine. Would you like to speak to her? Background rustling. *Sit down, sit down* and someone says *for the love of Jesus.*

-- Hello, yes this is Susan. No, mom, this is Susan.

--I'm still trying to get a ride out of this place. It's very difficult getting anything done. But I'm working on it. I'll be there when I can.

--I dreamed I was lost in a strange city. I needed a cab to get home. Two pale women wrestling with a baby stared but did not respond when I asked about a cab. I entered a hotel through the restaurant. Large men in brown suits jostled me. They were not unfriendly. I approached the registration desk, but the light was too bright to see anyone above. I began to ask, when I heard children getting ready for school.

--What are your pet peeves or things that make you frustrated or angry?

--What significant experiences, if any, have greatly affected your life? (For example, celebrations, traumas, world events).

--What type of physical contact from the people around you makes you uncomfortable?

Before:

"My mom loved to play word games
and assemble puzzles. She had an
excellent memory for faces, and events
that happened long ago."

After:

"Mom tries to disguise it, but I can tell
by this quizzical look that she gets on
her face when she cannot recognize me."

Before:

"Dad was the type of guy that everybody
loved to love. He kissed and hugged us all
the time and would even cry when we watched
a sad movie."

After:

"Dad cries and moans a lot and needs
a great deal of reassurance. He has a
tendency to cling or grab on to certain
members of the family."

Based on your loved one's current situation, our staff would like to
know what makes your loved one:

Smile
Laugh
Angry
Calm
Frustrated
Afraid
Cry

[*Sure I get frustrated.* George W. Bush]

ARDEN COURTS

Burial Arrangement

Resident's Name:
Responsible Party:
Funeral Home:
Phone Number:

--I've never seen anyone fight so hard, Maureen says. *It's as if she won a 15-round TKO.*

--Please indicate your name if completing this information on behalf of the resident.

posted by Susan at 3:35 PM 0 comments

Wednesday, August 23, 2006

Alzheimer's is one of those cataclysms that seems designed specifically to test the human spirit. Sherwin B. Nuland, *How We Die*

--We say *look forward to* and we say *look back.* The first suggests desire, *I look forward to seeing you,* but the second requires the confirmation of *in anger* or *with nostalgia* or *in time* to give it credence. (It's not adjectives we so dislike in poems, it's the judgment they offer before the crime is solved, as if the noun were presumed guilty of its qualities before they were assigned.)

--Sherwin B. Nuland, whose name compresses hope, describes the end of an Alzheimer's patient's life: he is tied to a bed so he will not wander; he forgets how to eat or drink; before he loses language, he forgets what it means. *The trains are not on time, do something!* comes to mean *tie my shoes.* He becomes comatose, he gets infections, and then he dies. *The End.*

--When is the future not forward, then? *Look Forward in Anger.*

--That the past is not back is a given. Karen says mom was angry at her for visiting when the cab might arrive to take her to Ohio. If she lives now in the past, in what tense do we write the present or the future, when mere reversals don't work either?

--Can I say I look forward to my mother's death? I would be assured she does not suffer. Or is there suffering in that state, which, if not directly felt by her, is commentary on *us*? If she uses Afghanistan as a word, and I know it as a war zone, can I not still say she suffers for being there—apart from where she is? When is a word only a word? When is a word no longer a word? When does *Ode on a Grecian Urn* become a sound poem? When is Keats Khlebnikov?

--Can I say I look forward to her death without wanting it? Not as desire but as fact. No, I cannot say that yet. It's that word, *yet*, that keeps us, not from despair but from act, even when that act makes sense. Nuland admits to *breaking the law*, easing his patient's pain. *I want to make sure they know not to resuscitate*, Karen says, as my mother would not want that. She did not want that when she could still imagine it.

--*Show Radhika your monkey face*, I tell Mom. She pushes her lower cheeks out with her tongue. For just a moment she plays.

posted by Susan at 3:44 PM 0 comments

Tuesday, August 22, 2006

--There have been *no incidents,* Karen reports. Phone message from Arden Courts: *your mother is doing fine, don't worry, she's even made a couple of friends.*

--My mother is an involuntary poet. Who is there to workshop her verses, refine her craft, edit her lines? *We have lots of activities for the residents here.* Banality as buffer to the mind's excesses. A banal art intended, if not to heal, then to restrain (I ought to say embrace, but cannot).

--The house. Toward which no sentiment, but. I cannot think about the house this week, I tell Bryant. The poem is my house, but I am estranged from it. She would sit in the dining room eating potato chips, waiting for the mail to come. *A poem communicates,* my students say, but I wonder *what?* He likes them to rhyme; music makes them memorable. Community, common: the response was not commensurate with the attack. Com- words break under the strain. The author is not dead but sits in the gazebo of the common area, behind a high chain link fence, painted green, and wonders why she has no audience. They nod, but she knows they do not understand her, the *normal people.*

--I think she might get better and go back.

--Radhika sees Ursula's mother-in-law, pushed by her son in a chair on little wheels. She has a flower tucked behind her left ear, plumeria I think. *She's not wearing pants; she's got a diaper!*

--Sangha thought learner chopsticks looked like a baby wearing a diaper. He'd yell *diaper!* in the restaurant when Bryant folded the paper cover, wadded it between the sticks, worked the rubber band around it.

--Beauty, even when its ugly. There, I stole that, but it doesn't mean I'm a plagiarist. In poetry it all comes down to percentages, as in baseball. Stephen Joyce will not give the scholars his grandfather's words because they (the scholars) would desecrate his memory. Now that's a different story.

posted by Susan at 12:02 PM 0 comments

Sunday, August 20, 2006

--Her voice is stronger this a.m. *I was watching a good show about wild animals.* Still needs a ride home, hard to find, but no mention of war torn countries, or trains, or a dead brother and their mother to look for.

--My local colleague's uncle threatened to sue if he found himself in his nephew's books. Students ask what they can and cannot write about their families, whose feelings to hurt, whose to leave alone, what might hurt, what not, whose names to use, who would surmise what, how to get around it all. Ethical issue #53. I wrote half a book about my mother, but never told her.

--Lissa tells me *the work* may divert me from grieving. *The work* is ethical issue #25, harvesting organs before a death, making hay at dusk rather than profoundest dark. The *I* an ethical burr—the cat would lick it, chew it, spit it out—a complication within #25, to say nothing of #53. Let us give the *I* #51, the number we want retired, as it belonged to Willie McGee. He is not I, but I will take his number to represent the lyric mode, the slap single to any field, the running catch, the stooping gait.

--An mp3 of my voice on the internet (from 2002), reading a poem I wrote in my mother's house one winter (1996 perhaps). The voice is placid, the tone wry. The poem wanders, weaves. Something about a "lack distracter" causes me to giggle.

--I play roles. I am "the good daughter," "the strong daughter," the "writer," member of the "sandwich generation" (*let's make a mommy sandwich!*), "tell-all-without-confessing-a-damn-thing poet," "chronicler" (in the sense of "historian"). She took me to see Mercedes McCambridge as Medea, the child-killer. My mother was horrified Medea was so fey. She walked on tiptoes, wore velvet slippers!

--Her strong voice made her ideal to portray hard-driving women, the obit reads.

--And so this evasion: one has wept at the sound of the voice (which is true) saying what cannot be true (her mother has gone for three days). The evasions must be mine, not hers. They must exist only in the composition. She will be composed, whether she is she or I.

posted by Susan at 3:35 PM 0 comments

Saturday, August 19, 2006

Telephone call:

--*I'm in a nursing home in Afghanistan and I need to get home to Wooster, Ohio; I need to find a train. I have my checkbook and you know I can take care of myself. I'm so glad you called; I don't have anyone's number. I might be on the road for a few days, so you won't hear from me. Have you heard anything about Mother? How's Joe?*

--*She's fine, she's fine. Would you like to speak to her?* The tone of voice people used with the demented. High, excited. *You need to sit down before you speak on the phone.*

--*Your calls are important to us.* I punch in the number 7.

--A young Bob Dylan reads a street sign about dogs. Runs words through paces. Statement. Question. Absurdity. Nature poem. Language poem. How do we use the word *lost*? She has *lost* her mother. She has *lost* her keys. She has *lost* her mind. Sangha thinks the *loss* of a family at the mall is like the *loss* of the family into which you were born. Thinks *pick up* means *adopt.* We will pick up the turkey. We might eat our child. Radhika grew agitated when we ate tortillas. Our cat, Tortilla.

--What is the function of the word *Afghanistan* in the statement above? It is far away; it is dangerous; she has never been there before. *Wooster* is where Joe, Mary and Karen lived, and Mother in her old age. Karen (my cousin) wonders at the *back story.* They visited her grandfather once or twice a year, but never spoke of him otherwise. My mother has not said a word about her father; he is still dead.

--I have not asked what she would say to her mother and to Joe. *Joe was drinking too much, and I told him he had to stop.* Always the declarative. My father was the one who doubted. And who believed.

--She sounds like my mother. She is more surprising than my mother. There is meaning there, but its range has narrowed. Our mother tongue is wandering, needs identification, a number. How can you sound the same when you are not?

--The names remain, however. Wooster, Afghanistan. There's history there, and it's not just hers.

--Her home recedes; no longer Virginia, it is now Ohio. She is living a fairy tale of origins. Like many tales, it contains no happiness, only struggle. Gretel has no Hansel now. Her house is bound to be eaten soon. If the house contains her mother, she too will be gone. What once was sugar is now ruin. *Once.* "I'm not nostalgic because I'm unhappy," I tell Bryant. A demented nostalgia, misplaced upon the future past (her childhood within her present, projected). *I really need to take grammar, but I don't have the time* my student says.

posted by Susan at 11:04 AM 0 comments

Friday, August 18, 2006

August Eighteen--

p.m.

--Karen left her at Arden Courts without saying she was going. Mom gets too upset when you leave.

--She was calm enough to go with Karen, once the doctor signed the papers. *It's the same floor plan as you saw in Fairfax.* She's in Evergreen House. It was a trip to see the doctor about her leg.

--Think of a few items she might want there. If they don't fit in the car, we have someone who helps with relocation.

--The brown chair covered by a green towel. Leather on the seat cracked and torn. Her reading lamp. *The Washington Post* (between 4-5 a.m.) has already been requested. Remember that she also likes to deliver it to her neighbors. The small TV upstairs. She has her bedside radio. Take away the checkbook, the financial papers, put them in a box, and mail them here. The neighbors can turn her lights on at night before we get a timer. She has several pairs of glasses, her meds (which she refused to take from Mohama). A couple of sets of clothes. Seasonally inappropriate. Her old sweater (my old sweater with holes in the arms—or is there another?). A plant from the garden. Pictures of her grandchildren.

--I got the nurse. She'd spent hours with mom. *She grabbed my arm. She's been baking brownies; we have lots of activities here.* Mom baking brownies in a care home. *She's eating dinner now.* Keeps saying she's got to go home. Past the caregivers, the nurse, the administrators, through the locked doors. *We've heard all about you—her daughter in Hawai`i!* She passed me on to the psychiatrist. *She'll be ok; she's just in shock, not knowing where she is.*

--Images I cannot assimilate, like the brownies.

--I've been making chapbooks. The front cover (green, white, with some black lines) is of a hand holding a pistol; the pistol is aimed at half the face of a smiling boy. Put the pages inside the two covers, then turn the Chicago screws to hold the book in place. Bryant is cutting the kids' hair upstairs. I ran out of books to make about the time the Cards beat the Cubs, 11-3.

--I drove over the Pali and back to get the book ingredients. There was no memorial to the man on the blue motorcycle, though there are flowers where a truck lost control and killed the old Vietnamese woman and her family. Farther down the hill toward town. *The motorcyclist killed on the Pali has been identified.* He was Matthew K., of Kailua, age 30. I drove in the lane he died in. Williams, the housewife, autumn leaves.

--Pres. Bush said in a press conference that the judge who struck down NSA wiretaps *doesn't understand the world we live in.*

posted by Susan at 3:43 PM 0 comments

Friday, August 18, 2006

a.m.

--The phone rang at 5 a.m., but no one heard it. At 6:15 my email read there's been another crisis; we're moving Mom as soon as the Dr. can sign the papers. Called Karen, her voice edgy. She was with mom, who'd taken an Ativan for her. She doesn't remember attacking Mohama in the night, trying to strangle her, threatening to kill her. Details from across the street, where Mohama fled. *She was so mean to us,* Eleanor said (later phone call). *Said I don't have her best interests at heart.*

--Milt will go with them to the Arden Courts in Potomac, if she's agitated. They might say she's going to see her mother and her brother. *That seems like going too far,* Bryant says, considering the cruelty of it. She won't remember.

--Maybe they are there.

--*She's always talking about her brother, Sangha,* Radhika's teacher tells us.

posted by Susan at 10:56 AM 0 comments

Thursday, August 17, 2006

--Mom has been more calm, though she did not get more zyprexa, as Mohama misunderstood the new dose. She still calls out for Mother, but with less panic. She tells Karen that Bryant and I are *good partners,* that she misses the kids. Mom ran yelling from the house this morning, refusing to bathe.

--I remember her only as a vibrant and interesting woman.

--Maureen writes *not to burst our little bubble.* Comfort is, as Jean Amery writes, *a play of the mind.* But also temporal play. If she behaves well, we can wait to move her to a *home.* Not first home, or second, but in the sense of imprisonment (enhomement?), necessary at that. Her wandering refigured as trespass, as escape, as harm to self and others. Her leg still hurts from the last fall, though nothing shows. So much refuses to show, is her mind and ours, not so much at play as running the same track, like dogs before they're saved from the slaughter.

--No one dies in the present. Depends on how you define the word *dies.* The man on the blue motorcycle died instantly on the Pali. My mother forgets what distinguishes an instant from a decade, three days from 40 years. Her mother left three days ago.

--Radhika's first tooth came out; her mouth filled with blood that stained a paper towel, the images of fluffy cat and fluffy dog. *You know what's really awesome,* she says, just before she loses it.

-- If you read what is written as it is published, you read in *real time.* If you come to it *after a time,* you are reading from the present into the past. You read back into memory, rather than toward the future that promises more writing. You read as an old person remembers, if their memory works, not yet unspooling what had been the present and the past into a new tense. The demented tense.

--As long as she lives in her own house, she will wonder why she is not the boss.

--The manner of my mother's losses (keys, self) versus those of my children (skateboard, the *when I was a kid* self). If I wrote my sentence right, I could perhaps make these losses commutative. The most beautiful lies are beautiful because they are grammatical.

--It's not so hard to lose these things.

--Even conservatives are daring to ask questions about Bush's intellectual capacity, says Joe Scarborough. The Freedom Agenda. Birthing pangs. Why he read Camus's *L'Etranger* on his vacation. All I remember is that *maman est morte* and someone got a telegram.

posted by Susan at 3:46 PM 0 comments

Wednesday, August 16, 2006

--Ah, so much better! Mohama says, *she's not wandering so much. I only let her go out after 9.* The meds must be working. Things change so quickly, Ursula said, *you don't know if you have four hours or four weeks. We've had two days.* Window not of clarity, but of relative calm.

--Mom remembers my kids, my husband, my work, if none of them by name or noun. She wants to know where her Mother is. *Have you heard? Has she ever done this before? I guess I shouldn't be worried, but I am. Let me know if you hear?*

--Yesterday, on the Pali. Police motorcycles threaded three stalled lanes of traffic. An accident covered two of them. Six policemen in a row waved us past, like a nursery rhyme. Shiny blue motorcycle down on the road, large white sheet blossoming beside it. Turned on NPR. The 66 year old man, a solitary academic, retired to Lebanon to grow tomatoes. His friend found him dead. An Israeli artillery shell broke through the wall of his house. What Voltaire did not know about gardens. A young woman wept, an old woman refused. Her husband and son dead in 1982. The Israeli novelist lost his son the day before the ceasefire, after calling for an end to the war. The motorcyclist was 31, the paper says this morning at 1:30, after the cat called out.

--Her mother lives in the future; she has gone but can perhaps be found. If only she will send a message, say where she is. The old woman, my mother, folds her past into future. Where we see her future as a short space, she knows it goes as far as her mother has traveled. It's been days since she left, and those days are in the past. But the worry that summons her into presence (I worry about her because she is now here with me) keeps going forward, which is back, which is only not still. This is no bridge into time; it is a train in the tunnel that has forgotten to stop. It is the blur of movement without the subtitles, or even the original, if unintelligible, tongue.

--To tell her the truth only agitates her. *Your mother is dead, mom,* doesn't work, because later she comes back into mind, alive in her being missing. It is another idea of death, that someone has gone without saying where. And they do return, as idea, as echo. My mother has no ideas; she has only persons, places, objects. She takes out the trash, collects the mail. There is the pulling in, the rejection of. Intake, output. But even in that narrow digital space, the 0s and the 1s are code.

--To participate in her fiction offers no consolation either. *I'm sure she's ok, that she'll come back.* Worry has always been how she knows what matters. Worry measures time, if not balances it. Worry is the metronome that keeps our pace. Her walking is its other measure. Pace, pacing. Concern's prosody. Its effect on the others. I could feel adrenaline in my chest.

--Jean Amery: *I had to invalidate consolation.*

--Consolation is not for the person who suffers, even if she's sometimes unaware of her suffering, or of its exact nature, or its meanings, its origins, ends. Consolation is not for the witness in the immediate moment, the one who performs the roles as they present themselves: caretaker, truth teller, fictionist, daughter, mother, author. Consolation exists, if it exists, in the act of description, which gives my mother back to herself, though she cannot read it. *Imagine...* my father would say, not a poet. He would shudder; better that shudder than unawareness. Consolation is not in the feeling better, but the feeling with. Death can end that (though I feel for the man on the motorcycle, I cannot reach him). Dementia is its foyer. Please come in. If empathy be bad faith, come here.

--*I'm not afraid of death any more,* says Mr. Ellis, Irish school counselor. *Don't get me wrong, I don't want to die, but I see it more clearly now.* His mother died at 92, sharp until 7 minutes before she passed. *Yes, we had a wake, but none of us drank (because we all drink, you know) and we didn't listen to music. She wasn't a music person.*

posted by Susan at 12:46 PM 0 comments

Monday, August 14, 2006

--Mohama bargains. She offers mom 10 minutes when she asks for 30. Lets her out for the paper at 8, not at 4. *She's ok this morning.* Says it's unkind for the neighbors to tell me about every crisis. *I'd rather know than not,* I say.

--Bryant says he wants the grandfather clock, then says he could always get another grandfather clock.

--*Your mother was so lively and alert,* Linh writes, *but that was five years ago.*

--Bryant wonders if it's really her mother she's looking for. Mother and brother. We get used to speaking of facts (it is a fact she looks for them) as overfull containers. The symbol in a sippy cup, failing to spill over only because of trademarked sippy cup technology. Yet she had a mother and a brother. Ask what they were going to do together, Bryant suggests.

--Günter Grass was a member of the SS. How many onions must he peel now? Can he weep on his own, all these years on? *He no longer has any moral authority,* a moral authority is quoted as saying.

--I push gently at Radhika's covers. Her arm emerges, finger pointed. *Red day!* She wears a *Soy flamenco* shirt and red shorts to school.

--Sy Hersh writes that Beirut is a test drive for Iran. They made their case to Cheney, and Bush followed quickly behind, then Condi. They will claim victory for Israel; they will bomb Iran. Anyone opposed to administration policy supports the terrorists. Hallucination behind the eye. *The birth of a new Middle East.* Truck plastered with images of abortion, a child's translucent head, mass of blood without breath. There are images no one in this country has seen of Lebanon, Iraq.

No leader of the Khmer Rouge has faced a court of law.

--Email from Karen: Mom slept.

posted by Susan at 12:09 PM 0 comments

Sunday, August 13, 2006

--1:40 p.m. The phone rings. Caller ID: Frederick W. Schultz. She hasn't called here in months. *Have you seen my mother? I don't know where she is. She's been gone for three days now and it's not like her to leave and not to say. They won't tell me. There's a woman staying here with me, but I don't know where my mother went.* Then some chitchat about the kids, my work schedule. *I really don't know, mom. I don't know.*

--Email: 5:30 a.m. HST, from Maureen. Mom hasn't slept. She left the house at 5 and knocked on Milt and Eleanor's door, then went to Connie's. She called the police, wanting to get rid of the aide. Karen was over. She needs to be moved.

--Called Mohama. Mom had taken the phone with her when she left.

--We left the house. With two days before my car was to go into the shop for a new head gasket, it overheated going up the Pali. The cooling system was flooded. Car towed. Tomorrow we know if it's worth salvage.

--Home to email from Karen. Mom was calm, charming, by the time she got there. Invited her in for instant coffee and potato chips. She wants the key to her house. She does not understand why she cannot have the key to her house.

--She follows people out. She confronts them in the garage. She wanted the key. I told Karen Bryant would leave without saying to avoid her anger. One upset better than two, he'd say.

--The zyprexa's been doubled, and is to be given at night. A second aide will come in this evening so the first aide can get some sleep. Karen's afraid this will freak mom out. But if Mohama disappears downstairs, she may forget she's there.

--Time is an emulsion, Ashbery writes in his fence-sitting poem. *La boue.* My mother's mother is as alive as Sangha's brother, Thurney, though Sangha's calls his brother *imaginary* now. My mother's mother is stronger than her daughter's imagination. She is. And she is missing. And I've been tasked with finding her.

--I met her once, when I was Radhika's age. I remember a porch, and a small bridge. I remember my mother saying something about *100 years ago,* and wondering if she'd known Abe Lincoln.

--I think I remember that. When I went back to where I thought we'd been decades later, I found the bridge, but not the grandmother.

--But my grandmother has returned. She is not in Pennsylvania, or Ohio, she is not the woman who screamed in the middle of the night, or the woman who demanded support all her life from a daughter who left at 15. She is not the woman on the porch, wiry and old as my mother is now. She is with my mother, and that is how we know she is missing (again). My mother asks me questions, and I want only to answer them. *She'll be back, mom.*

--*It bothers her sometimes she can't remember.* And then she falls back on simply not remembering. She hands off the baton to us. The baton is a question passed over and again until the line is found, and we dare not let it drop. That would mean the race is lost.

posted by Susan at 5:23 PM 0 comments

Friday, August 11, 2006:

Two

--Papers scattered around the house are covered with names. Susan Bryant Radhika Sangha Tortilla. Some of the letters formed backward, especially the s's, even when Radhika makes the symbol for "money" ($). She knows the power of the written name. She paints rainbows, and at the top she writes Radhika. *It's for my teacher.* I am still Susan to my mother, but other names, however installed in print, have dissolved.

--I told him that elegies are like vacations, death and ease the only times we Americans permit ourselves to contemplate meaning.

--*She is looking around the house for her mother and her brother. We said they went away on vacation together and asked Mohama to stay with her. Telling her the truth agitates her more.* It's the fictions ease things, for a time. One minute, or twenty. Sometimes a day, even.

--*She didn't say, you lead, and I'll follow. She held my hand.*

posted by Susan at 5:22 PM 0 comments

Friday, August 11, 2006

--Ursula's mother-in-law was watching too much CNN. One morning she began kicking and punching her daughter-in-law, yelling *I know what you're thinking of doing! I should have known years ago! Get away from me!* (Andrea Yates) No more CNN. Asked what she wanted for breakfast, she said, *a hamburger with everything! Filet mignon!* (Food channel) And then there was the week of babies. *How are the little ones?* (Baby channel?)

--There are windows of lucidity. You won't know when and you won't know for how long.

--Mohama tried to bathe Mom, wash her hair. Mom went to Milt and El, *gave them the riot act,* told them (times 5) she's been on her own since she was 15. She bathes every morning, she said. Maybe she should move to Hawai`i, where Susan can care for her.

--You wonder what to do within those windows, what their clarity means, whether it is real, or no. Lucidity comes back as the real. *How much is zero? Nothing,* says Radhika. But when it goes, what is real then? How are we to take the *as*? An architecture of ruins, great wall beside a KFC. My students wanted to find *the truth,* and for once I sympathize.

--The only time she got drunk, my mother said, she pounded her fists into her bed and yelled, war is hell! *Wawa danced naked!* says Radhika, remembering my poem. That must have been the other time.

--One woman had her lip gloss confiscated. Bombs made of sports drinks, brewed on planes, waves of them falling into the sea. *She was a member of the Hemlock Society,* Ursula says, as was mom, says Eleanor. Dreams of suicide, of what would be at least a limit. In her moment of lucidity she said, *I know I came here to die, but I didn't know it would take so long or be so hard.*

--The situation itself is the poem; you need only take it down.

--Ursula, who doesn't have children, bought her mother-in-law a sippy cup. She wanders the baby sections of stores. Looks for *tools*. Drives to Costco and Walmart, gets diapers, baby wipes, frets about the waste, the literal waste. *She would say to put her in a home, but it's Dave and I who can't face it.*

--*I hate the racist things she says!* She knows a psychotherapist who nursed her mentor as she died. This woman who had traveled the world was, for two months at the end, a bigot. I say how hard it is to parse the sentence you believe from the one you throw away, the voluntary from the involuntary impulse. *I think of everything that is possible with a knife,* Bryant says, *and I ask the children to step away.* That quarter of a second of knowing is our buffer. *What is a buffer?* Sangha says, and I point to the iron knobs at the back of the train.

--There is an umpire in us, all dressed in white and black stripes, and he's itching to blow his whistle, though we ask for quiet when he comes upon our darkness. I hit three batters yesterday and I don't know why it keeps happening but there's a genie (ungenial, at that) in me who keeps tipping my wrist like a faulty signal at an intersection. No, that was Anthony Reyes.

2. Email

--We'll wait for her appointment next week with the psychiatrist before we start making any decisions about moving/taking another step.

posted by Susan at 3:08 PM 0 comments

Thursday, August 10, 2006

a.m.

--First talk with Mohama. *She's my grandmother!*

--She wanted to go out in the rain. She did not want to be followed. She did not want to use an umbrella. She wanted to have dinner with her daughter and grandchildren. She is better now.

--*I wish I could see you more often. Maybe I should move to Hawai`i.* [Pause] *Just kidding.*

p.m.

--"*Death is the no-response,*" Levinas writes—*the absence of responsive and receptive keeping open. However, death is also a question* (via Stephen Collis). If death gives us the open-endedness of no-response, a space in which to pose our questions, a utopian lack of moment, then what (end?) point is dementia? Surely it cannot exist in an opening or a closing, is a door ajar, or seeming to be ajar. Yet the question you pose is not the question that is answered. Is non-sequitur, malaprop, bad prop for a play in which the chairs do not even look for their author. The author is not dead, is demented, neither at nor away from home, but wandering. In her shoe is a label, marking her name and number. Only at the airport will they think to take it off, find her name.

--He claims that poetry is response, not agon, is reciprocity, not taking. Yet the demented poem cannot reciprocate, even if it adds on. It is a labyrinth with no end, but many paths. She will take them all, and then take them again. *Let her wash the clothes three times a day; it gives her something to do. Besides, she wasn't washing at all before.*

--The website cites a scientist who has found *cleaner cells* that wear out over time. They are the body's janitors, and when they retire, the mind is junk. When asked who had *word power,* only the 2nd grade girls raised their hands. She might also say she has that power. Not remembered but invented out of the circulation of trash, Yankee Stadium, circa 1998. Or Candlestick. When she started to forget her stories, she said they no longer mattered.

--*The man on the dump.* If there is a voice behind this it is his. The poet of the imagination keeps intruding out of reciprocal non-space, the nook into which we shoehorn our guests. And I keep meaning to say but. But but.

--Sangha learns to add with his invisible hand. It lies under the paper, gives him a headstart of ten fingers, against which he places the visible hand. 8 + 4 requires a hand and a half. Is not 14, but 12.

--Today, her first day, Radhika learned about the number 1 and the letter A. Take us, yes, take us back to the beginning. We will count our letters with our invisible hands.

posted by Susan at 6:19 PM 0 comments

Wednesday, August 09, 2006

4 a.m., Kāne`ohe, with cat, Radhika.

--Called Sara from the Newark Airport with four quarters, which made for five minutes on the phone. Mom had taken the key, left for Connie's in the middle of the night. *You can't force me to stay in my house.* The key was in her pocketbook, which she'd clutched as we left (old brown purse with two false leather handles). But the pocketbook was missing. *Do you have my key?* she yelled at Sara. *Where is my pocketbook?* Found in a closet.

--Reports that Condi (*Condi is doing such a good job*) is furious at the President. Too many people died in Qana. Pat Robertson calls Ehud Olmert *cool under pressure,* wishes Americans had the fortitude of Israelis.

--We contemplate a return, sooner, later. Whether it will be my trip, or ours.

--Mohama moves in today. Sara (*the creature*) leaves. Radhika: *I love you, Sara.*

6:30, a.m.

--We call mom to say we're back. *It was so nice to see you; the visit went well, don't you think? I have to have a new caregiver and I don't want that.*

--*Mom, you need someone in the house with you.* As if repetition worked against repetition. The repeated phrase might wriggle into a moment of lucidity, remain long enough to last. She might think it again, not as repetition, but as fact.

--The demented person's lapses in speech—at dinner, while walking—are not pauses for reflection, though they sometimes seem so. They are not musical rests, nor are they spaces within which she listens. They are still places, not winter but something far less green.

--The poet's lapses, whose form is the space between observations, offer reflection as possibility, what Lissa says is missing from our discourse. The demented person does not recognize herself in the mirror, thinks she is someone else, her own mother perhaps. She does not understand language, laughs at jokes when others laugh. There is give without take, take without the gift of speech. *Democracies are peace-loving nations; freedom is universal; there is no civil war in Iraq because people there voted for a non-sectarian government.* Reflect on those sentences, those without hesitation, without rest. Tell us whom you see. Who's the most beautiful of them all?

--*I keep thinking if she just gets the right care, she'll get better.*

3. Email 1

--Karen says mom was looking for her mother, but then realized she was dead. Said it must have been the mother of her son she was looking for, her son Joseph. (Joseph was her brother.) She has two daughters, Susan and Mary Ann and hopes to visit Susan in Hawai'i again some day. (Mary Ann was a friend.)

--Sangha has drawn a picture of himself in red teeshirt with a bull on it, standing on a skateboard. The wheels are in perspective, but not the boy.

4. Email 2

--Milt says mom locked Mohama out of the house. Says she came over yesterday with the key, said she wants the doors open so she can come and go. She said Susan and the kids were there, they'd just finished lunch. Went downstairs to look. We weren't there.

1:30 p.m.

--A place (not a state, but not really a place either, a placelessness) beyond ethics. Ethics requires enough memory that forgetting is transgression. Then kindness is not ethical, though we wish it were.

--Coming out of depression, I saw both the randomness of my thoughts and the necessity of assigning them value. *Have you had any spiritual experiences lately?* was code for psychosis, or so I guessed. Is there a spirit within dementia, if not a system of belief, then its flickerings, its necessary failures? Is its only belief paranoia, its only doubt a rooting for lost keys? Can spirit not, at its source, be this literal? A neighborhood for those who forget, leaving traces of their forgetting in what we remember? The quality of what I remember, its syntax, the image of a woman with wet matted hair lying on a doctor's table demanding to settle her accounts, is not what I have wished, but that I remember it makes it stay. You stay waiting. Staying [is] power.

--If *writing is an aid to memory* (Hejinian), then can it un-likewise be an aid to forgetting? Can each word so uncore the word before that we are bereft of syntax? If syntax survives (for now), can it not take us forward, or back, or only here and there? *Are we there yet?* the kids ask, and we say no, we are not there but we are here, which is where you asked. This place falls away like highway rest stops, so nearly alike we might yet approach them, albeit under new names or management. The Vince Lombardi stop was always last.

--And if writing is an aid to forgetting, then why take this down as dictation, rather than reshape it in some other form? Form that marked it as poem, as line, as refrain (since dementia is the refrain of her life, at least)? Form that demarcated the difference between this life (demented as it is) and this poem (moments of forgetting tethered into some shape)? Because dementia is where the form and the life collide, where hallucination consumes form. Dementia is absence of form, absence of form /content rift or incorporation. Dementia is (though it is not) the poem in the process (or lack thereof) of forgetting poem.

--Hence our reliance on documents: reports by the Guardian ad Litem, brief by the lawyer, papers to sign, papers to notarize. Where biology meets dementia, there I adopt you, my mother. Whatever genes we share are now subordinate to a judge's decree. It is the form of these documents that gives us leave to approximate the old order, to install caregivers and to take them away, to settle our accounts (those most literal, and least). You cannot shout so loud as to take away the power of these forms.

posted by Susan at 5:46 PM 0 comments

Monday, August 07, 2006

a.m.

--Mom fell in Connie's backyard next door, cutting her right leg.
Before she was found by a woman with a black dog and an SUV,
John Kerry sticker on its bumper, the sprinkler that she had fallen on
began shooting water on her. We took her, drenched, to Immediate
Care in McLean, with a set of dry clothes and a green and brown
towel.

--Her legs are white and thin, skin papery, covered with bruises and
abrasions. On her shoulder more abrasions, her back bent forward,
the spine crooked, as it has always been. The new pants didn't fit, so
she pulled the dry yellow top down over her waist.

--She wanted to pay the bill. She wanted to know how long *that
creature* (*I can't remember her name*) would be around. She wanted
to know how much we'd paid her. She wanted to pay her. She
wanted to pay the doctor. She had her checks with her. I tried to hide
around the corner, but the receptionist told me to stand where mom
could see me. Mom got up, wanted to show her Medicare card. *They
don't take insurance, mom, we have to file papers later. How do I
always get into these messes?* she asked.

--Sangha walked next door to Connie's, cried when he thought
everyone was gone.

--*Your neighbors are lucky to have you around,* the doctor said to
her as he applied the butterfly bandage to her ankle. *Does she live
alone?*

--There were four chairs in the waiting room in front of a tropical
fish tank: yellow tang and clown fish. We played musical chairs. The
chair across from mom was vacated. A large-bellied man with gray
pony tail sat down, teased my mother by saying he might take her

chair. *You look like you need two chairs,* she said. The man across from me winked.

--*It'll be nice when you leave; there won't be so much talking.* She makes the sign of talking with her hand. *The house will feel so empty without you.*

p.m.

--Red Roof Inn, near BWI airport. Drove here through thunderstorms that wound Sangha up like a spring, as Radhika slept beside him.

--*He is trying to run my life,* she said angrily, as I heard Bryant say something about court papers. Sara is staying until Wednesday. Sara rushed back in the house before Mom could lock the door on her. Angry woman in a suburban garage. *Calm it down,* I said (having ended our last family trip by yelling at her in the garage to *TAKE CARE OF YOURSELF*). Bryant had grandma pose at the door with the kids, took their photo. I gave her a second hug, and we pulled out.

--*That was better than last time,* Bryant says. *I took her picture with her grandkids.*

--Remember to put in the change of address form. *All bills please* at the top.

--Remember to get access to her checking account.

--Remember to call when you get back. She will want to know, even if she's angry. Even if you left her with *that woman.* Even if it's quieter now.

--Discuss the relative advantages (such as they are) of therapeutic lying and telling the blunt truth. *I had to tell her the truth at the end. I told her she has dementia. She said something about 'a home' when I walked with her after she fell. She knows, somewhere she knows. She's heard it enough times.*

posted by Susan at 5:12 PM 0 comments

Friday, August 04, 2006

Apologies: this is out of sequence.

--The first was The Gardens at Fair Oaks, just off Lee Highway in Fairfax. Mickey, the woman with Tidewater accent, said it was near Wagman's, a *new grocery store we're all excited about.* The Special Care Center (unit for Alzheimer's patients) was located underneath the regular assisted living facility, beside a huge hole in the ground, apartments-to-be for those who did not yet need to be assisted. Later in the day someone referred to them as *the basement people.*

--The décor was suburban bourgeois. The drapes, the wallpaper, the mock-Victorian furniture. Like rooms at the Mormon Temple in Lāi`e, it insists on visual conformity, even as it suggests comfort. Like my mother's living room, it is static, refuses change. Aids to memory. We assume *it* ought not change.

--*It matters to some people that we don't have fancy chandeliers. Would you rather have a fancy chandelier, or good care for your parents?*

--Each wing of the unit had a name. Country Cottages. Bird Sanctuary. Another had to do with the sea. At the entrance of each was an alcove with décor appropriate to the wing. There were fake birds on a fake trellis outside the sanctuary. Outside each person's door was a *memory box,* with photos of the resident and his or her family. Residents were engaged in an activity in the common room. A West Indian woman named Hazel tossed a ball at them. One woman had on a huge straw hat. Others turned smiling gazes toward the children. Hazel's voice did not change when she turned from the old ladies to the children.

--Most of the care workers are African or Latina. All the residents are white. *What happens when there aren't enough immigrants to take care of all the old white ladies?* Bryant asked.

--The second place was Arden Courts. We had a hard time finding it, but it too was on Lee-Jackson Memorial Highway in a different part of Fairfax, beside new townhouses. The street names were Peaceful Creek Drive and Blissful Valley Drive, like bad names for military operations. Operation Enduring Freedom replaced Operation Infinite Justice.

--There was a Lee Jackson day, until the commonwealth of Virginia added Martin Luther King to it. In some places, Lee Highway becomes Washington Street.

--There used to be rabbits there, our guide told us. More memory boxes, but this time a garden. The doors are only locked when it gets dangerously hot. There are over 70 activities a week. Behind the nursing station there's a beauty parlor.

--Our guide asks us how we met. Radhika laughs.

--We gave the second place a deposit, put mom on the waiting list. I cannot see her there. I cannot see her here. I cannot see her anywhere.

--"The good son" visits his mother every other day. They sit together in the garden. The garden forms a circle around the building. If you leave from one place, you cannot but arrive back. You cannot wander.

--The memory box cannot resemble a Cornell box. Its objects must resemble the person whose box it is; they must be easily identifiable, they must seem to be in their place. That place can harbor no dissonance or absurdity. Where art would be, there is the assertion of a past that cohered, though it led them here. Where life would be ordinary, would follow, there is leakage, randomness. Or do I merely hope?

--The memory box is a memorial before the fact (before the fact of death, though not of alteration). It contains within itself the notion that what it contains has been mostly forgotten by the person whose box it is. It is, then, a box of forgetting, record of what has already slipped away, must be contained within the thick frame, the surface glass. Forgetfulness is a state where nothing is contained; it flies. Memory, we think until we see it lost, remains.

--*Would you describe yourself as an optimist or a pessimist?* There is a "lifestyle biography" to be filled out on behalf of the person entering the home. *Do you speak another language? How do you want to be addressed?* Or: what have you forgotten of another language? Would you have called yourself an optimist despite all evidence to the contrary?

--For the native speaker, the state of not understanding a sentence spoken on the radio or in a crowd is normal. It does not worry the native listener. For the second language speaker or listener, this not understanding presents itself as disturbance. It represents all that is not yet learned, absorbed, cultural material that has not been explained.

--For the person with dementia, the state of knowing is itself disturbance. Hence the anger, or the perplexity, or the blankness, or even the smile. There is, for a time, a sense that something is amiss. My mother saved an article from the newspaper by George Will on his mother's dementia. What knowledge was there in that act?

--*She did nothing all day and got paid for it.* One works for pay and work is an activity. To sit and watch over is not work because it is not an activity. *She makes me sandwiches, watches TV, and sleeps all day.* The Puritan work ethic survives illness. Thrives on it.

--*She should just take a cab and get away.* She would stand outside the shower while Sara bathed and say she was calling a cab. She went to the neighbors to ask for the phone number for a cab. No one told her. She told me to call a cab. I have never seen my mother take a cab.

--*I don't have a car anymore, you know. It's a real problem. I have to get rides to the store from my neighbors.*

--She will not pay for services, though she would eat the food brought by neighbors and take the rides offered and ask them to do her taxes. *I am nice to them now, because I'll need them when I'm old,* she would say.

--*When she made demands of you, did you give in or did you fight back?* Hard now to defer, deflect, count on her diminished memory to smooth things over. Time may not heal, but waiting sometimes does. She cannot hold on so long. Though resentments return, they also fail.

--"Blood pressure medicine" = anti-anxiety medication.

--Radhika's head is wet. She leans it back against the couch. *It's bad for her hair and for the couch.* I get a towel to place behind her head. She is still leaning against the pillow. Mom walks over; I tell Radhika to move her head. (This is not the dementia.)

--On reading back, I fear I have reversed details—what we saw at The Gardens versus what we saw at Arden Courts—and I wonder if it matters what I got right and what wrong. The poem is a memory box. It's best if these memories move, but only in certain ways. You must be precise, I tell my students, even when you appear to be uncontrolled. There is nothing breezy about this moment, but there might yet be use for precision.

posted by Susan at 5:00 PM 0 comments

August Six

p.m.

--Just past 8 o'clock. Sangha and Radhika chase fireflies around the back yard, catch them in folded hands. They move slowly, sit on Sangha's hand, flashing on and off, in green.

--At the Hirshhorn, Radhika and I watch *Wie die Dinge laufen,* made in Switzerland in the late 1980s. I think it means, *why the things laugh.* It's translated *How things work.* A bag of trash spirals lower and lower until it hits a tire that rolls and hits something else. Half an hour later, gallons of liquid and muck have spilled, candles have fallen over and lit up puddles of gasoline or explosive devices, little carts have crashed into obstacles that set off more consequences. The entire event performed with throw aways, plastic bottles, old tires, black balloons, crudely yet precisely crafted wooden carts, and bags of trash. *It's a sculpture,* a woman mutters to her husband as they walked past.

--Most of Lebanon's beaches are covered in crude oil.

--My mother's obsessions: managing accounts (her checkbook); picking up newspapers and delivering them to the neighbors' doors; collecting the mail of neighbors who are away; having coffee with Connie, who's been away; and taking out the trash. She takes out the trash as soon as it's "made," sometimes a single orange peel or used coffee filter. Sometimes as we are adding trash to the bag, as we promise more to come.

--We put out a bowl of salad for everyone and she took it.

--She emptied the remaining salad (at dinner's end) into the cup of salad dressing, the better to keep both.

--Sangha and Radhika watched her watching TV upstairs.

--She is asleep; the kids chase fireflies. I can hear their voices and those of the cicadas.

--Mom says it will be *very sad* to see us go. And will our *hired help* come tomorrow, and why?

--In one memory card I alluded to Leslie Scalapino's obscurity as coming from her intent to see without mediation. Mediation left to the reader, while the poet lists perceptions before they can be thought. What of the moment of that transfer from thing perceived to perception monitored, negotiated, filtered? The children shout with delight, almost past the point of my hearing them. That is the moment I want to attend to, give care to, kneel down to place the bandage over, fussing over drops of blood or pus, suggesting they might mean something, I cannot yet know what.

--*Are you an optimist or a pessimist?* Questions lodged in the present, as if it were (still) continuous. Which tense is optimistic, which pessimistic? My mother wrote a check to renew her membership to AARP for the next two years. I suspect she forgot to mail it. Forgetting is the optimist.

--Will she forget her fears, or do fears come after forgetting, needing no subject to anchor them? The children ask about lightning, about thunder. Body before mind, sight before sound, sensation before filtering.

--Diana came over today with her dog, Buster, a corgie. Mom was happy to have him wander the house, sit on the couch, sniff the carpet, eat the crumbs.

--*Where did the dog go?*

posted by Susan at 6:10 AM 0 comments

Sunday, August 06, 2006

--*Joe Lieberman is the last honest man,* writes Robert Kagan.
Meaning his mind is still, it will not change, unbending honest.

--*Change mind,* one of Radhika's early favorite expressions in
English.

--There is no poet of dementia, nor will there probably be one. But
the question remains of how to attend to its repetitions, its failures
of completion, its half-steps. Imagine a form for dementia, where
habit is confused with ritual, obsession. *Your mom's behavior is
predictable,* Bryant says. *She gets angry when we leave.* So we back
out the driveway quickly, not looking up to see her wave us back.
It's a sick little economy, but it's an economy, Bryant says. *One upset
is better than two.*

--My Spanish teacher began to correct us into mistakes. She heard
attender for *assistir* so often that she mistook the former for the
latter. Repetition is artificial memory, though it sometimes sticks. (I
had written the subjunctive, my favorite tense.)

--Within the realm of prediction (what she will do and when)
there is predication, moments hinged on other moments we cannot
know unless we know her well. I become her concordance within
this discordance, referring back. Where narration fails, the lyrical
moment (Mama, Fred, house) can still sustain its meaning. The lyric
cannot utterly renounce its loveliness, even now. *Where is Pa going?*
where *Pa* stands for *Bryant.*

--We wonder when this began. Many of these traits pre-existed me,
the outbursts of anger (though she used to absent herself, afraid
of what she might say), the intrusions, the fierceness. Was it when
rituals replaced retrospection? Was it when she stopped being
interested in politics? When she decided this Bush *wasn't so bad?*

When she stopped bathing? When she stopped changing her clothes? How far back can we measure an illness that does not bruise the skin, which cannot be excised? How can we measure it against anxiety, depression, her unnamed companions?

--Sangha has been watching a show about cavemen, their drawings. He has his pile of stones, his game boy. Radhika writes lists of words, our names, the names of TV characters, her S's inevitably mirrored.

-- If dementia is endless repetition, then how to write it down without altering it, so that it is at once legible to the reader and varied enough for her to absorb it? What is the prosody of dementia, and can it vary without altering what it is? Look at it. Really look at it. To find meaning there is to flinch. To flinch is to make a necessary sound of this.

posted by Susan at 6:29 AM 0 comments

Saturday, August 05, 2006

a.m.

--You are developing a fascination with your mother's decline. You
begin to anticipate her speech patterns, their inappropriateness. The
comment you fear will be racist. The statement you fear will not
acknowledge your children as yours. Her anger at the *mess.* You
fill in the gaps yourself, until your own mind grows addled, if *grow*
is the word you intend. The mind turned inside out, gray sock (not
matter), whose contents are discontent, brain nailed to a table that
will not stand still. Neither brain nor table. Let these thoughts settle,
the toxins seep into the water table. If you drink them again, you
might not know, until your body sprouted something alien to it.

--Residents may bring their own furniture to the home, or use the
furniture provided.

--I tell my students to leave out the I, to write about their subject, not
themselves. We are the least interesting of our subjects. We know too
much, or too little. *Don't say that, you'll become part of the illness,
too,* says Sara, when I apologize for my mother's behavior. But am I
not a part? And can I not resist commentary, its calming, my pet rat
rooting for meaning? Scant reward.

--The man with the blue guitar would have much to say about this.
His couplets might uncouple imagination from its incursions into
the real, unmask the myth of dementia as an illness that removes us
from imagination's reality. But the man with the blue guitar lacks a
face, a voice; he is all that the poet makes of him. My mother has a
face, though she cannot save it, and her voice, though it carries less
freight, still fills the rooms of her house. If the man with the blue
guitar were to forget how to play it, or its color, then we might be
getting somewhere.

--I wonder, is there a philosophy of aging? A consolation of it?

--Mom settles her accounts. She finds some few receipts. $24.99 for the black shoes with pink highlights we bought for her at Payless. *Those were expensive,* she says, as she adds the amount in her frail handwriting. *Where are the grocery receipts?* she calls down the stairs. Bryant would have them, I say. He says you have them, she responds. *I'll write you a check for $50 then,* she adds. *She might not have left the house that day without her checkbook in hand,* Linda tells us.

--How to prevent her from writing checks. Scenario one, rejected by the agency, was to take the checkbook when we leave. Scenario two: change my address at the Post Office, as my name is on most accounts. She has pasted check 2003 into the space for 2006. I once found lists of her accounts from well before I was born, amounts for breakfast, for lunch, for rent, for light bulbs.

--Williams hated the uses of old words to describe the new. Robins were robins because Puritans already possessed that word. They knew the words, not the images, placed word over image like translucencies. Mom calls Bryant Fred, though she recognizes the disjunction. *Did Fred leave in the car?* A slight pause to denote her own awareness that that was not the word, but it came closest. Our names are our functions.

--She calls her names. It's not the her that is Sara, but Sara's function. She watches. Mom does not want to be watched. Her old binoculars sit by the phone. She used to point them toward the neighbors, when there weren't birds enough to track.

--*Your mom has now written two checks for $250. She wrote one, then five minutes later she wrote another.*

p.m.

--When we returned from the museums, Mom wanted to settle accounts. I said Bryant knew how much we'd spent on groceries. But he says you know. She said she'd write a check. Bryant said she had, and showed her the check she'd written in the morning. Only one of them.

--Eleanor called to say that Mom had been angry at Milt, but was *amazingly lucid* yesterday. *She knows what's going on in Russia.* I wonder what is going on in Russia.

--Is there a *Dementia for Dummies*?

--How would it define words like *knowledge,* or like *wisdom.* Let alone *safety* and *comfort.* At the end, comfort is our wisdom. The philosophy of consolation. The minor fictions that give us another hour before worry's onset, if we're lucky.

--*Is that creature woman coming tomorrow?—Martha, that is rude; you shouldn't say that about people. Sara is coming tomorrow.*

--Sangha wonders what the words *cease fire* mean. We watch news of rockets and bombings, see bodies taken out of ruins. Rice says there is no civil war in Iraq; there are sectarian tensions. When the reporter mutters, she allows that *some of the tensions are violent.*

--*I have never said anything overly optimistic about the situation in Iraq,* says Donald Rumsfeld. *You'd have to look like the dickens.*

posted by Susan at 6:27 AM 0 comments

Friday, August 04, 2006

August Three

--*Our enemy has a brain.* Donald Rumsfeld.

--A man is killed while riding his bicycle in front of his house. We are given crumpled bicycle tires and the bottom of his white shoe, its parallel lines.

--If you strike us, we will strike you, and if you strike us back, we will strike you again.

--At dinner. *What happened to his mother?* "Whose mother?" *The boy's.* "I'm here," I say. *Oh.*

--There is Plan A, which is not working, and then there is Plan B, which we suspect will not work. *She is past strategizing.* Which is not to say that we are not, simply that our strategies will fail unless, a) the psychotropics kick in, and/or b) a new caregiver, one who is quieter, less obtrusive, can break the cycle of abuse. *She used to find your hot button and press it until it drove you crazy,* says Bryant. We are searching for her cold buttons. Her tender ones.

--Her name is Mohama. I'm thinking nothing short of Mahatma will suffice.

--Figures of speech. Something having to do with two facts becoming a single invented irreality. She remembers her past, but forgets that it is hers. She has forgotten my past, replaced it with hers. It does not quite fit, and yet it cannot quite not fit, either. When she sees that the car is gone, she asks, *where's Pa?* That was our past, yes. The one I remember.

--So that this figure is not metaphor, or simile. This figure is not metonymy. Perhaps it's catechresis, though I've never liked that word. This is literal fact that becomes figure because it falls apart. Metaphor creates: this figure makes new what has fallen apart. When told by the county that the large stones in his front yard went against the codes, the man claimed in court that he was using the architectural style called "ruins."

--What you missed in her was her charm. *Oh, I know, when my sister brought me food one day, Martha was out in the front yard inviting everyone in...I couldn't say anything to my sister about your mother anymore.* "Your mother is beautiful," a rental car employee told me once, as mom paid my bill.

--We get labels to iron into her clothes. They say *Martha.* They give a number of identification, and a phone number. In case she wanders.

--She remembers my name, my face. She does not know Bryant's name, though she knows who he is. The children swim in and out of her awareness. Sangha puts a shoe on his head, or a shoe box. He might get dirty playing on the floor.

posted by Susan at 5:33 AM 0 comments

Thursday, August 03, 2006

a.m.

--At breakfast, Mom says she had a horrible dream. *I was being mean to everyone around me, and it was today.*

--*I was being mean to everyone, and I couldn't get over it even after I woke up.*

--Dementia as poetic form. Reverse Stein: not insistence, but repetition. Repetition as diminishment. Nothing accrues. Sentences do not stick to each other; the mind is humid, deflects meaning as something that becomes, as a post-it note flutters off a solid surface. Meaning happens only as instances of it tear apart. Analogy to the administration's sense of audience. *She'll be gone in two weeks. You'll be home in a week. The corner has been turned. It's just the dead-enders.* And then again, in time. As if assurance were all we need, because we cannot remember wanting something to happen now. Or that now is all there is, subject to air currents, whims of moods that rolodex (if that word still exists, if it is a verb).

--*Mama was much smaller than I am. I don't remember myself as a child. I don't think I was a good one.*

--Sara arrives. *I thought we were through with this.* "Two weeks," says Bryant. He is learning the art of distraction, deferral, the putting off.

--Sangha and Radhika play outside my room. Rules are born as they occur to them. Their instabilities are delight.

--On leaving, mom walks us into the garage. *How long is goofus here for?* "Who's goofus?" *The one I call goofus.* [Mom called me goofus when I was a child, but there was lightness in her voice then.]

posted by Susan at 6:31 AM 0 comments

Wednesday, August 02, 2006

--Grandma Wawa was yelling. She might yell at you. She was
yelling at Sara, who said Mom had done the laundry three times
today, each time with fresh soap. Mom screamed she did not like that
as Sara skittered to the laundry room.

--My mother's power has always come from her anger. It used to
come equally from her charm.

--Do you remember the time you spent with your grandmother? my
mother asks me. *No, because I never knew my grandmothers,* I say, *it
was you who lived with your grandmother. You didn't know Mama?
No, she was your grandmother, not mine. My grandmother was your
mother. That just can't be possible.*

--I hardly remember my brother at all. I never knew my sister.

--She often confuses us. She told Bryant I was born in 1917, which
is her birth year. She was born on the day of one of the Russian
Revolutions. She tells me now that I went away to school when I was
a child. I wonder what happens to her past, once it becomes mine.

--We went to the lawyer, who became our therapist.

--There are inventories and reports, but don't expect an answer from
the County. The lawyer's father, a retired lawyer, recently received a
response to an estate filing from 1987.

--The kids were in the back seat of the car performing "the news."
*George Bush bombed people and children died. George Bush is in jail;
if he acts good, he can get out again. Some Iraqi soldiers were killed.*

--Sangha's dramas are often violent, yet his tone is so cheerful you have to listen for the words.

--Tyson's Corner Mall, where we went for shoes. The mall of my youth. Then it was one level, outdoor parking, nothing fancy. Now two levels, hundreds of shops, inside and outside (the "boutiques"). Altar to American excess. The kids grow hyper, want things. We bought mom a pair of shoes that are too small. Sangha's shoes, sporting both laces and velcro, fit.

--*Maya and Miguel is sponsored by No Child Left Behind.*

--The kids made pipe cleaner bracelets and pirates while we talked with the lawyer. She told us about her neighborhood in Arlington, much coveted for its proximity to the Metro. When Bush became president, the area flooded with Texans. One woman read the deeds to the area, the ones that still say "no colored, no Jews." She saw no bars in the neighborhood. *It's because of zoning,* the lawyer said. The woman from Texas thought this meant citizens of the area did not approve of alcohol. She tried to set up a chapter of the Christian Women for Temperance in Arlington, Virginia.

--*Like most women of her generation, she is probably a racist.* My suspicion is that a better word is "misanthrope." Resident of an all-white neighborhood for many years, she tried hard not to be racist. Martin Luther King, Jr. on Meet the Press, circa 1966 or 1967, speaking out of the old wood piece of furniture that was our radio. It was the neighbors who said they didn't want Negroes around.

--*I don't want to see your face. She cackles. She steals my money. She wouldn't know. Your sister can't get herself here on time, can she? Imagine anyone cackling like that any more.*

–Sunrise Assisted Living: A Special Neighborhood for the Memory Impaired.

posted by Susan at 6:30 AM 0 comments

Wednesday, August 02, 2006

8 a.m.

--Mom is wearing a Kailua Surfriders Staff teeshirt this morning. That must be Bryant's old shirt. No, she insists, it's an Iowa teeshirt. The young man down the street, the one she's never met, gave her an Iowa teeshirt when he heard she'd gone to Iowa. It's Iowa.

--I didn't know she was coming today.

--She was sweet at 4 a.m., Bryant says. They had the first conversation about the shirt then.

--Israel sends more ground troops into Lebanon. *There's an opportunity there,* we read in the Washington Post.

--I don't like you. I don't like them. I don't like them either. And Susan? She laughs.

--Compare and contrast the acquisition of a language to its loss. Avoid the trap of merely saying that the latter happens in reverse order of the former. You are likely to do better if you see them as similar processes, though one leads to gain, the other loss. Think chemistry. Think performance of a script. Think *Harold and the Purple Crayon.* Think Harold Pinter.

--Think two old men fishing for a beautiful young woman in a lake. Think one of them might get "lucky."

--When are you leaving? Where are you going? Are you taking the kids?

--Sangha and May hatch plots of their own. Go quiet when I arrive. In this life, you either make plots or have them hatched around you. Like eggs. Like poisoned ones.

posted by Susan at 6:46 AM 0 comments

Tuesday, August 01, 2006

My 16th anniversary in Hawai`i, celebrated in Virginia.

Mom:

--Shown a photograph of herself and Sangha (2 or 3 years ago), she doesn't recognize herself. *That's my mother,* she says.

--She looks around the house for her mother; asks the caregiver where her mother has gone. Gets on the phone to ask someone else where her mother is.

--When her mother died, she told me casually as we drove through Alexandria, days after it happened. I was in elementary school, wondered even then (especially then) why she expressed no emotion. Said she only wished her father had *been a better father.* He died before I was born, of alcohol, mostly.

--On our second day we go to Costco, in Sterling—the exurbs, full of strip malls, townhouse developments, mini-mansion areas, Versailles on Route Seven, at least three mega-churches with parking structures, one with two American flags as large as any attached to a car dealership—and, on our return, mom thinks we just arrived. *What a surprise!*

--*What is your name?* she asks Radhika.

--*She's not my grandma!* says Radhika. We explain to her that she has two grandmas, that this is the one she doesn't see very often.

--*What was Africa like?* Bryant asks mom. *Can't say that in one sentence. I'll let you have three. It was very pleasant.* (She was there during the second World War, told stories of ducking in ditches to avoid bombs, of seeing a dead body in a trash can.)

--Wants to know where the bottle of glue is. Needs to put stamps on an envelope. We explain that she can lick the stamp. She wants to cut stamps off an old envelope and put them on a new one. The new envelope has a miscellany of bills and announcements in it. I say we'll buy her stamps today and she can use them tomorrow.

--The power of tomorrow or even of an hour from now. Of later.

--To deal with a person with dementia you need to take a fiction workshop. How to tell the truth, but tell it slant. *Therapeutic lying* is what the agency people call it.

--Mom took the keys out of the door yesterday. At 4 a.m. Bryant found her pounding on the inside door to the garage. She opens the garage door at 4 every morning for the newspaper people. Sara gets up at 4 to open the door for her, but she is not here at night while we are visiting.

--The keys are the central characters in many of our fictions.

--To take Bush's *freedom is on the march in the Middle East,* or Rice's *we can't have a ceasefire because we want a change in the status quo, which leads to a lasting peace.* To take these and so many more "sayings," and reduce them to metaphorical rubble. *Poetry can kill a man,* wrote Stevens, though I think it's not so much the men as their mutterings we need to kill.

--Cheney was seen in a D.C. Borders buying a book on armies.

--Mel Gibson blames everything on the Jews. How original.

--The arc of my mother's life, from adventure and danger to the suburban fortress, from work to its refusal. Too serious about her parenting, there were too few accidents in my childhood.

--*Parts of your mother are working pretty well today,* Bryant says just now. *It makes her less happy,* he adds.

10 a.m.

--Mom goes for a walk. After 15 minutes I go in search of her. She's seated on a bench on someone's porch at the end of the street. *When are you leaving for the day?* she asks. I return to the house.

--After another 15 minutes, Sangha and Radhika and I head out with a bottle of water for Grandma Wawa. She's no longer on the bench. So we go to Connie's house, on the other side of mom's. Connie is away; usually, mom opens her door with the key and makes her coffee, usually in the morning, sometimes in the middle of the night on one of her wanders. Mom's there on the porch. I tell her Sara will be late because she's been stuck on the beltway for two hours in traffic. *What I went through to get that woman out of my house,* she says, *and for you to invite her back. Mom,* I say, lacking the therapeutic lie, *you've got dementia, and you can't be in the house by yourself. They're all telling stories about me,* she responds.

--And then the kids demanded cereal. More cereal, more milk.

12:30 p.m.

--What followed was anger. High decibel kine. Agitation, disturbance. Followed later by a quiet lunch. The cycling is fairly quick, as if years of our lives were streaming by, unimpeded by obstacle of clock or historical fact.

--I can't decide if it's the details that are moving, or the larger fact of her absence from us. She is still "herself," as one says, but lacks the anchor of consistent memory, or even the anger she used to sustain for days. *Why is Wawa so angry?* asks Radhika.

--The great generation, the one that refused weakness, aid, whose retrospection is more historical than personal, because introspection is a weakness.

--*How do you spell butterfly slowly?*

6:55 p.m.

--How do you spell slowly? The day has been slow, with many shifts of mood. As we left for Lisa's, mom was telling me that her caregiver had stolen from her (and more). On our return, Sara said she and mom had become *good buddies.*

--She told the man up the street on whose porch she sometimes sits that her heat wasn't working right. Virginia this time of year is over 90 degrees each day, the air thick with humidity. He came by, checked it out, told her the heat was working just fine.

--The best policy is to say yes. If she says, *call your sister and tell her to take you home,* you say yes. If she says, *call a taxi and get that woman out of my house,* you say yes. I said *no.* She screamed at me: *Whose house is this anyway? How dare you say no to me!*

--How to govern my tendency to repeat myself. The pull back, the desire, not for revenge, but for intervention, to say (again) what is wrong and what is right. Of course you trust your mother, even when she's not "right." Of course you trust her.

--We force her to take medications she never would submit to taking herself. That they would have made her better then means only that now she is slightly more calm in her askew-ity.

--The old episodes of rage return in their clarity, but do not make more sense than they had. In this instance, the effect cannot explain the cause. Does dementia uncensor the tongue, like alcohol? Or does dementia cause an utterly new violence? Does the demented person mourn her *loss of culture,* as Lissa puts it? Or are her mind's chemicals suddenly awash in the substance of anger itself, merely attaching to specific objects, ideas?

--Alan, who suffered an early dementia, would get angry, and then sweet, would forget, and then be acute, at least for a time. The intellect, before it goes out, returns as paranoia, as anger, as interpretation that can only reveal one's own weakness, against which only the will seems an appropriate weapon. The words still come, and they still mean things. But they do not mean the right things.

--Acute neurotics always create the circumstances in which their greatest fears will be realized.

--Mom's caregiver Sara lost her son to a brain tumor earlier this year. *The smell of blood in the hospital.* She gave him injections, because she had to, though they had made her sick.

--She's lost even the dream of suicide.

--None of this is new. Dementia is bricolage, is collage, is mixed-up syntax. It is nothing new. To describe it is to say nothing new. It cannot be analyzed, because its origins, and its ends, cannot be located. The maps are hanging from laundry lines in a humid country; the ink that is their roads has dripped off the dark paper that had enclosed them.

--Sangha calms himself with "the air force." He flies two paper airplanes around the room for an hour, making their sounds himself. Beside the Pentagon three huge blue curved spikes are going up. A memorial to the Air Force. Franco could devise no more gaudy monument. Elsewhere, a Marine Corps monument will be built. *I support the troops.*

--With age, the world becomes more literal. Then curves off into the no-time of the old mother playing hide-and-seek with her dead mother. Where is she? And if she were to find her mother, what then? They who never could abide.

--Sangha's drama emerges from the bathroom. Radhika and Bryant chant about rice in the pot, three days old. We called Tiare, who says Tor slaps her on the cheek each morning at 6 a.m. Who only eats with company.

--*Have you taken my keys? Have you taken my phone? Are you eating my food? Are you stealing my money? What are you still doing here? When are you leaving?*

--*And so what do we do?* Some of us tell fart jokes in the back seat, or tell us that we smell, or make childish pacts, or play jan ken po with both hands at a Mexican restaurant. And others of us watch those who play jan ken po and are content that such moments are still possible. Just don't look at tomorrow's newspaper.

--*Why is six afraid of seven?* Joseph asks. *Because seven eight nine,* he answers.

posted by Susan at 6:44 AM 0 comments
About Me

Name:Susan

View my complete profile

Links

* Google News
* Edit-Me
* Edit-Me

Previous Posts

* August 31, 2006 --"She looks good, calm, frien...
* August 30, 2006 --Form follows dysfunction. (L...
* August 27, 2006 --Yesterday we could call out, b...
* August 25, 2006 --"We want the mind to last," L...
* August 24, 2006 --"She's fine, she's fine. Wou...
* August 23, 2006 Alzheimer's is one of those cata...
* August 22, 2006 --There have been "no incidents,...
* August 20, 2006 --Her voice stronger this a.m....
* August 19, 2006 Telephone call: --"I'm in a ...
* August Eighteen-- p.m. --Karen left her at Arde...

Powered by Blogger

Susan M. Schultz has lived and taught in Hawai`i since 1990. She is author of several volumes of poetry, including *Aleatory Allegories* (2000) and *And Then Something Happened* (2004) from Salt and *Memory Cards & Adoption Papers* (2001) from Potes & Poets. The University of Alabama Press published her book of essays *A Poetics of Impasse in Modern and Contemporary American Poetry* (2005) and *The Tribe of John: Ashbery and Contemporary Poetry* (1995), which she edited. She is editor and publisher of Tinfish Press out of her home in Kāne`ohe, where she lives with her husband and two children. She is a lifelong fan of the St. Louis Cardinals.

Singing Horse Press Titles

Charles Alexander, *Near Or Random Acts*. 2004, $15.00
David Antin, *John Cage Uncaged Is Still Cagey*. 2005, $15.00
Rae Armantrout, *Collected Prose*. 2007, $17.00
Julia Blumenreich, *Meeting Tessie*. 1994, $6.00
Linh Dinh, *Drunkard Boxing*. 1998, $6.00
Norman Fischer, *Success*. 1999, $14.00
Norman Fischer, *I Was Blown Back*. 2005, $15.00
Phillip Foss, *The Ideation*. 2004, $15.00
Phillip Foss, *Imperfect Poverty*. 2006, $15.00
Eli Goldblatt, *Without a Trace*. 2001, $12.50
Mary Rising Higgins, *)cliff TIDES((*. 2005, $15.00
Mary Rising Higgins, *)joule TIDES((*. 2007, $15.00
Lindsay Hill, *Contango*. 2006, $14.00
Karen Kelley, *Her Angel*. 1992, $7.50
Karen Kelley, *Mysterious Peripheries*. 2006, $15.00
Kevin Killian & Leslie Scalapino, *Stone Marmalade*. 1996, $9.50
Hank Lazer, *The New Spirit*. 2005, $14.00
McCreary, Chris & Jenn, *The Effacements / a doctrine of signatures*. 2002, $12.50
David Miller, *The Waters of Marah*. 2002, $12.50
Andrew Mossin, *The Epochal Body*. 2004, $15.00
Andrew Mossin, *The Veil*. 2008, $15.00
Paul Naylor, *Playing Well With Others*. 2004, $15.00
Gil Ott, *Pact*. 2002, $14.00
Ted Pearson, *Encryptions*. 2007. $15.00
Heather Thomas, *Practicing Amnesia*. 2000, $12.50
Rosmarie Waldrop, *Split Infinities*. 1998, $14.00
Lewis Warsh, *Touch of the Whip*. 2001, $14.00

These titles are available online at **www.singinghorsepress.com**, or through Small Press Distribution, at (800) 869-7553, or online at **www. spdbooks.org.**